COMPARATIVE STUDY OF THE ASSIMILATION OF MEXICAN AMERICANS:
PAROCHIAL SCHOOLS VERSUS PUBLIC SCHOOLS

by

Philip E. Lampe

San Francisco

1975

Printed in 1975 by

R AND E RESEARCH ASSOCIATES
4843 Mission Street, San Francisco, 94112
18581 McFarland Avenue, Saratoga, California, 95070

Publishers and Distributors of Ethnic Studies
Editor: Adam S. Eterovich
Publisher: Robert D. Reed

Library of Congress Card Catalog Number

75-18128

ISBN

0-88247-359-X

TABLE OF CONTENTS

iii

LIST OF TABLES

ABSTRACT

The objectives of this study were twofold: to discover to what extent the Mexican American has been assimilated into our Anglo society in San Antonio, Texas, and also to ascertain whether this social process is more or less successful or pronounced in the public school system as compared to the parochial school system. It was believed that the resulting empirical information about this relatively neglected minority group would be of both theoretical as well as practical importance. The resulting data can be utilized to provide some needed tests of the many theories regarding assimilation.

Milton Gordon provided the theoretical framework for the investigation. Gordon maintains that there are seven types or stages of assimilation, each of which may be thought of as constituting a particular step or stage of the assimilation process. These seven types are (1) acculturation, (2) structural, (3) amalgamation, (4) identificational, (5) behavior receptional, (6) attitude receptional, and (7) civic assimilation.

Eight hypotheses were tested, based on the preceeding types. It was predicted that there was no relationship between each of the seven indicated types or aspects of assimilation and attendance at either a public or a parochial school. An additional hypothesis stated that there was no difference in the degree of overall assimilation between the Mexican Americans in the public school system and those in the parochial system. This study was limited to eighth grade Mexican American students. The sample included 383 students, 168 attending nine public schools and 215 students from nine parochial schools.

Degree of assimilation of Mexican American students on each of the seven types was measured by means of a seven-part questionnaire. This instrument was specially designed by the investigator based on the literature. Data were statistically analyzed to test each of the null hypotheses. Hypotheses were accepted or rejected based on the results of Student's t test. Only those found to be significant at the .05 level were accepted. The Mann-Whitney U test was also used and the correlation between the results yielded by both tests was .939.

The following are the central findings of this research:

1. There was a significant difference in overall assimilation between public and parochial school eighth grade students.

2. Parochial school students revealed a significantly greater degree acculturation, structural assimilation, favorable attitude toward amalgamation, attitude receptional assimilation, and civic assimilation.

3. Public school students showed significantly more identificational assimilation.

4. There was no significant difference in behavior receptional assimilation between those in public and parochial schools.

Thus, seven of the eight null hypotheses were rejected. Data indicated that, in general, parochial school Mexican American students were more similar to the Anglos except in the way they identified themselves. There was some evidence to suggest that religion, directly or indirectly, was responsible for many of these differences, even though almost the entire sample was Catholic.

CHAPTER I

STATEMENT OF PROBLEM AND THEORETICAL ORIENTATION

Introduction

The concept of assimilation has received a great deal of attention and use by sociologists in the twentieth century, particularly with reference to the various immigrant groups in the United States. Although there is a general agreement about its importance, particularly in the study of race and ethnic relations, there is, unfortunately, no corresponding agreement concerning its specific meaning (Gordon, 1964:61-68). There is, however, a general agreement that it signifies some kind of a coming together or a movement toward greater homogeneity. The inevitability, possibility or probability that assimilation will take place has been of interest to many sociologists, especially those who have provided us with race relations cycles (Park, 1949; Bogardus, 1930; Glick, 1955; Brown, 1934; Rose, 1964), as has the questions of the speed and ease of the assimilation process (Schermerhorn, 1964; Warner and Srole, 1945; Rinder, 1965).

The degree and speed of this coming together are affected not only by the desire and ability of the minority group in question, but, as has been pointed out by Schermerhorn (1970) and Berry (1965), by the dominant group who may or may not encourage or permit assimilation. In addition to permitting assimilation to take place, the dominant group may even force it upon the minority group, at least under certain conditions, as Simpson and Yinger point out (1965:20-21).

In the United States assimilation has generally taken the form of "Anglo-conformity" (Gordon, 1964:88-114) or, as some refer to it "Americanization" (Berry, 1965:248; Vander Zanden, 1963:303). There are those, however, who argue that it has been of the type commonly known as the "melting pot" (Gordon, 1964:115-31). Milton Gordon also identifies a third type, in addition to the other two, which aims at achieving societal uniformity only in those areas where national unity is believed to be necessary, but where group differences are encouraged in other areas. This is known as "cultural pluralism" (1964:133-59). Whatever the form, however, it is quite evident that the process has not yet been completed.

Far from being a dead issue, or one of only speculative interest, assimilation of minority groups is considered a current and very important problem not only by social scientists, but also by the government and general public as well. Thus, the concept is a rich one which has provided the focus for many studies and theories in the past, and which, undoubtedly, will continue to do so in the future.

The Mexican Americans are at one and the same time both the oldest and newest of the American minority groups. Although they have been present in at least parts of this country, notably the Southwest, since these United States were formed, they have not received notice nationwide until recently. This lack of attention is reflected in the titles of a couple of articles which deal with them, namely "A Minority Nobody Knows" (Rowan, 1970), and "The Invisible Minority" (NEA, 1970).

Celia S. Heller (1966:4) wrote in the Introduction to her book that

...there seems to be a general agreement among interested social scientists that the field of Mexican American studies has been sadly neglected from the forties to the present day, although it did attract the attention of social scientists in earlier years.

Therefore, this researcher echoes her sentiment when she wrote that "the present study is an attempt to fill, if only partially, this gap" (1966:4).

Much of what has been written was based on old stereotypes which have just been perpetuated and passed on. These are now further from the truth than they ever were, but they form the basis of many Anglo teachers' knowledge of the Mexican Americans whom they have to teach (Moore, 1970:82-83).

It has also been pointed out, and is quite evident from the literature, that Mexican Americans are a diverse group and their situation varies from place to place as well as generation to generation (Grebler, Moore and Guzman, 1970:9-10). This being the case, we cannot, as social scientists, be content to rely for our knowledge on old studies, but we must be constantly updating and expanding our knowledge.

Statement of the Problem

Our American Creed promises freedom, equality and liberty to all peoples regardless of race, color or religious belief, and this Creed is tacitly accepted and respected--if not followed--by most Americans. This general acceptance should mean that all individuals and groups that so desire will be assimilated into our society. In fact, however, this is not always the case, and prejudice and discrimination abound.

Gunnar Myrdal (1944:53) has written:

In trying to reconcile conflicting valuations the ordinary American apparently is inclined to believe that, as generations pass on, the remaining minority groups--with certain distinct exceptions (notably Orientals and Negroes) . . . will be assimilated into a homogeneous nation. The American Creed is at least partially responsible for this, as well as for the Americans' inclination to deem this assimilation desirable . . . .

This long-range view of ultimate assimilation can be found to coexist with any degree of race prejudice in the actual present day situation. In many parts of the country Mexicans are kept in a status similar to the Negro's or only a step above . . . .

In spite of all race prejudice, few Americans seem to doubt that it is the ultimate fate of this nation to incorporate without distinction not only all the Northern European stocks, but also the people from Eastern and Southern Europe, the Near East and Mexico. They see obstacles; they emphasize the religious and "racial" differences; they believe it will take a long time. But they assume that it is going to happen, and do not have, on the whole, strong objections to it--provided it is located in a distant future.

The problem was to see if this assumed and, apparently, desired assimilation has indeed been taking place for the Mexican American in San Antonio, or if it is still a thing in the distant future; and to discover the part the school plays in this assimilation process.

Mexican Americans were chosen as the minority group in this study because they are the second largest minority group in the United States today. There are over five million in the United States, and in the Southwestern border states of Texas, Arizona, California, New Mexico and Colorado where more than 80 percent of them live, the ratio of Mexican Americans to Anglos is one to seven. Because of a much higher birth rate, however, the ratio of children less than 15 years old is about one to five (Moore, 1970:

2

53-58). Thus the problem of assimilation and intergroup relations promises to be even more acute in the future.

Nationwide, this ethnic group which has been termed by one writer a partial minority group (Howard, 1970), has only recently come to the public's attention after taking their cue from the Blacks. They have begun developing a group consciousness and initiated a concerted effort to achieve "brown power." Since the interest is new, there is still relatively little sociological literature concerning this group, although for the past several years it has been growing.

San Antonio was chosen because it is a large urban center, thus furnishing a setting which should be more conducive to providing opportunities for assimilation, and due to the fact that approximately 80 percent of all Mexican Americans are now urban dwellers it should be more representative of the actual situation in which they find themselves than would a non-urban setting (Moore, 1970:55-56). In addition, San Antonio is a city where approximately half of the population has some Mexican American ancestry, and because they are not new arrivals but have been there from the founding of the city in 1718, there has been sufficient time for the processes of assimilation to have taken place, or at least to be well underway.

The specific aspect of this general problem of assimilation of the Mexican American which was investigated is the role the school plays. Since more than 40 percent of the Mexican Americans are children of less than 15 years of age, the impact of the school system and the importance of the role it plays is far greater than would be expected for other ethnic groups, i.e., both the Anglos and nonwhites have a higher median age (Moore, 1970:57).

It was not at all clear, however, what influence the school exercised in the assimilation of its students who are members of minorities into the American society. There was reason to believe that the role the school plays in the assimilation of them would vary, among other things, depending on whether they were public schools or parochial schools. In an article which appeared almost two decades ago Broom and Shevky stated that "the church is the principle agency of cultural conservatism for Mexicans in the United States and reinforces the separateness of the group" (1952:154). They further point out that this phenomenon is not limited to the Catholic Church. More recently, Celia Heller accepted this and other similar opinions and stated that "there seems to be little doubt that the 'religious factor' (to use Professor Lenski's phrase) plays an important role in the rate of acculturation of Mexican Americans" (1966:19). This "religious factor" is highlighted in the parochial schools, especially in the grade schools which characteristically give more religious training to all their students than do high schools or colleges.

In speaking about this same topic Joan Moore wrote that "generally it is true that the Mexican identification with Catholicism acted to strengthen the already acute isolation of Mexicans from the predominantly Protestant Southwest" (1970:85). Later she stated:

> It may have been equally true that this very expensive system of
> parochial schools served not only to defend the faith but to main-
> tain the cultural and social distinctiveness of Mexicans, although
> no special effort to this end appears to have been made. In any
> case the hierarchy could keep Mexican children away from the assimi-
> lative influence of the public schools and simultaneously claim
> credit for efficient Americanization. McNamara sees the parochial
> system and the new but very limited sallies into social welfare as
> basically designed to defend the faith and not, except accidentally,
> to promote assimilation (1970:87).

Many private church-related schools are closing due to lack of funds and many or their critics are elated since it has been frequently stated that a public education is more conducive to the assimilation of its pupils to the American way. It was of special interest, therefore, to see if Mexican Americans in the public schools were in fact more assimilated than their counterparts in church-related privated schools.

Significance of the Problem

We are in a period of increasing internal strife and tension among the various racial and ethnic minorities which are components of our society. There are charges and counter-charges being made that contend our society and the American Creed is a failure and a lie (Rodriguez, 1970:135-40; Galarza, 1970:148-56). A great uneasiness and a growing militancy can be found among the members of the Mexican American community (Moore, 1970:148-56). Meanwhile, members of the Anglo community are resentful of the charges and threats, and unwilling to accept the contentions of prejudice and discrimination which are hurled at them.

All of this brings to mind the suggestions of Louis Wirth that minorities can be classified in a number of ways, but that in light of the contemporary world setting the most appropriate and meaningful criteria are the goals toward which the minority and dominant groups are striving. Accordingly, he distinguished between four types of minority groups: pluralistic, assimilationist, secessionist and militant. Furthermore, he claimed that these types could become successive stages in the life cycle of minorities under certain conditions:

> The initial goal of an emerging minority group, as it becomes aware of its ethnic identity, is to seek toleration for its cultural differences. By virtue of this striving it constitutes a pluralistic minority. If sufficient toleration and autonomy is attained the pluralistic minority advances to the assimilationist stage, characterized by the desire for acceptance by and incorporation into the dominant group. Frustration of this desire for full participation is likely to produce (1) secessionist tendencies which may take the form either of the complete separation from the dominant group and the establishment of sovereign nationhood, or (2) the drive to become incorporated into another state with which there exists close cultural or historical identification. Progress in either of these directions may in turn lead to the goal of domination over others and the resort to militant methods of achieving that objective. If this goal is actually reached, the group sheds the distinctive characteristics of a minority. (1945:347).

This alone gives sufficient motivation and reason to study the existing situation, but there is further reason provided by Yinger (1965:31) who writes:

> To understand a society, it is very important to know the goals of its minorities, the causes of those goals and the changes that are taking place in them. American minorities have almost always been assimilationist or pluralistic.

The majority of Mexican Americans by-and-large have shown by their words and actions that they too are either pluralists or assimilationists, but this could change if their hopes and aspirations are frustrated too long. The importance of hopes and dreams in the direction minority responses take in relation to the dominant group is also pointed out by Yinger (1965:11-14). It is the youth, where the aspirations of parents meet the realities of society which provides the social scientist with the greatest opportunity to study the probable future trends. This is especially true of this minority group which is composed of such a large percentage of young people.

The role the school plays in the assimilation process is important in itself. If the country is committed to the ideal that one society, with all minorities disappearing through assimilation, is our desired goal, then it behooves us to see if this can best be accomplished in the public schools and/or in the private church-related schools which are in the process of disappearing.

Definition of Terms

Assimilation

Since there are so many different definitions of this term, perhaps we would do well to refer to that found in the Modern Dictionary of Sociology, which reads as follows:

> The complete merging of groups or individuals with separate cultures and identifications into one group with a common culture and identity. In most sociological usage assimilation may refer to both the one-way absorption of an individual or group into another group and the mutual absorption or blending of divergent cultures. Assimilation is similar to acculturation, in which a culture is modified through contact with one or more cultures, but assimilation involves the complete elimination of cultural differences and differentiating group identifications. Unlike amalgamation, assimilation does not require a biological fusing of groups (Theodorson and Theodorson, 1969:17).

Mexican American

Most previous studies have used a Spanish surname as the basis for identifying a person as a Mexican American. Among other obvious weaknesses this method fails to identify those individuals whose mother is Mexican American but whose father is Anglo. Since the young child in the United States spends much more time with the mother than the father, she is generally recognized as one of the most influential of the socializing agents. Therefore, there is some reason to believe that a child from such an ethnically mixed marriage will be, or at least can be, as Mexican American as a child with a Spanish surname. In view of this, the investigator included in the category Mexican American all individuals who had at least one parent of Mexican or Mexican American ancestry.

Anglo American

The definition herein was employed in a previous study of Anglos and Mexican Americans, carried out in Texas under the direction of Texas A&M University. It reads:

> The term 'Anglo-White' is used here to denote the majority group in Texas--majority in terms of population, wealth and power. Anglo-whites are those persons who are not nonwhite and who are not white persons of Spanish surname (or ancestry) (Upham and Wright, 1966:25).

Our previous definition, which departed from theirs on the use of Mexican ancestry instead of Spanish surname in the identification of Mexican Americans, necessitated the inclusion of this factor in the above definition, as found in the brackets.

Public School

This term can and does apply to all levels of education, elementary, secondary or university, so long as "such schools are supported by general taxation and open on a common basis to all" (Rivlin and Schneler, 1943:165-66).

Parochial School

The term is commonly applied to "the schools under the control of the Church, and attached in some manner to the local system of parish churches" (Monroe, 1913:606).

Theoretical Frame of Reference

The concept of assimilation is a common one in sociology and any number of sociologists and other social scientists have offered a definition, as we have seen. Perhaps the most complete and comprehensive treatment of the concept is that of Milton Gordon, who points out that assimilation is a general term covering a multitude of sub-processes.

He sets forth seven types or stages of assimilation, each of which may be thought of as constituting a particular step or aspect of the assimilation process.

These subprocesses and the corresponding type of assimilation are:

1. Change of cultural patterns to those of the host society--Cultural or behavioral assimilation (acculturation).

2. Large-scale entrance into cliques, clubs, and institutions of the host society on the primary group level--Structural assimilation.

3. Large-scale intermarriage--Maritial assimilation (amalgamation).

4. Development of a sense of peoplehood based exclusively on the host society--Identificational assimilation.

5. Absence of discrimination--Behavioral receptional assimilation.

6. Absence of prejudice--Attitude receptional assimilation.

7. Absence of value and power conflict--Civic assimilation (1964:71).

Gordon indicates that conformity to all of the above would represent a situation in which the ultimate form of assimilation--complete assimilation to the culture and society of the host country--would be achieved. This is, then, offered as an ideal type, in the Weberian tradition, against which to measure a concrete example. The entire assimilation process is, therefore, a matter of degree, and each of the different stages or subprocesses may likewise take place in varying degrees (1964:69-71).

To be completely or fully assimilated, in the sense in which Gordon uses the term, would result in a situation in which "the distinctiveness of ethnic groups disappears and members of those groups become merged into a society without clear ethnic boundaries" (Rose, 1971:267).

Commenting recently on Milton Gordon's treatment of assimilation and the distinctions he has made, Jerry Rose (1971:267) states that, "there are cultural and structural aspects of assimilation. Culturally, a people are assimilated when the subcultural ways of life that distinguish them disappear."

Later, he continues:

> Structurally, assimilation has occurred when people from an ethnic group
> have been fully accepted as equal participants in the general social
> life of the society, one in which there is not a differential distribu-
> tion of the roles and statuses to members of different ethnic groups.
> The measure of structural assimilation is the ability of ethnic group
> members to move freely through the society, joining clubs, marrying and
> selecting places of residence without any hindrance because of their
> ethnic names or their known ethnic backgrounds.

> Gordon distinguishes between cultural and structural assimilation be-
> cause he, like many other sociologists, wants to point out that these
> two kinds do not necessarily go together (1971:267-68).

In fact, Gordon not only distinguishes between cultural and structural assimilation, as do others, but between each of the above subtypes. Every one of these are
related, of course, but are also, in a very real sense, independent. That is, they can
and often do vary in degree. A high degree of assimilation in one of these subtypes
does not ensure, although it may facilitate, a high degree of assimilation in another.

The first of these, acculturation, appears to be one of special importance,
as Gordon points out. It is in a rather unique relation to all the others in that it
can greatly facilitate or impede progress in all the other areas. However, as previously
mentioned, being acculturated does not lead automatically to any of the following types.
The Black experience gives ample testimony to this fact.

If there is one "key" type, or stage, in the overall process of assimilation,
Gordon indicates that it is probably structural assimilation. This one, it seems, more
than any other one, leads to, or at least is conducive to, progress in all the rest.
Apparently this view is shared by most racists who are particularly vigorous in their
opposition to structural assimilation, as expressed by their demands for segregation.

The dynamic relationship which exists between cultural assimilation and structural assimilation is cogently treated by Pierre van den Berghe. His conclusions are
consistent with those already presented above; however, his approach is from the opposite
direction. Van den Berghe (1967:135) writes:

> Cultural pluralism between ethnic groups cannot exist without institu-
> tional duplication and hence without social pluralism; that is, any
> form of cultural pluralism has a structural facet which can be treated
> as social pluralism.

He then goes on to explain that institutional or social pluralism can continue
to exist without a corresponding cultural pluralism, whereas the converse is not true.
Thus, the relationship between the two is asymmetrical. Furthermore, if structural
pluralism persists for too long a period of time, due to segregation, there is the possibility, and even probability, that some degree of cultural "drift" will result. To
the extent that this occurs, a culturally homogeneous society can become culturally
heterogeneous; this he terms "secondary cultural pluralism" (1967:135).

Large-scale intermarriage, or amalgamation, is viewed by many social scientists as the final proof, or consequence, of assimilation. This is to be distinguished
from simple miscegenation which frequently occurs in the total absence of assimilation.
The history of slavery in the United States provides sufficient evidence of this.

Some sociologists approach this phenomenon in a very different manner, such as Schermerhorn's use of the combination of centripetal and centrifugal forces (1970: 77-85). Much of the current theory regarding assimilation can be accommodated, however, within the framework provided by Gordon. Indeed, it is felt that the most commonly identified and ennumerated forces are to be found in the subprocesses indicated by him.

Assimilation has been seen by many people as a sort of panacea. The unification of all Americans was expected to result from the assimilation of immigrant groups, and this was considered to be one of the objectives of the public schools. According to the theory of the "common school", which gave rise to the public school system, the fact that all students from diverse backgrounds received the same nonsectarian education in the same schools would result in the assimilation of all people into a unified whole. Diversity, like unity, is seen as a product of learning, and the school has a major role to play in this area (Callahan, 1958:126-31).

Andrew M. Greeley (1973:198) recently pointed out that this idea still exists.

One of the main arguments for the public schools in the ninteenth century, and indeed up to the 1950s, was that the public school was supposed to be the primary agent of the melting pot; it was supposed to acculturate the immigrants - that is to say, of course, to make them WASPs. The public school was expected to eliminate "divisiveness" from American society, to provide the core of a common culture which all Americans would share. As recently as the summer of 1971, the columnist Gary Wills argued in support of busing that there was nothing wrong with using the schools as a means for massive social engineering, since integrating the society was no more an exercise in social engineering than acculturating immigrant groups.

Based on this theory, then, it would be expected, in the case of the present study, that Mexican Americans in public schools would be more assimilated than those in nonpublic schools. This result would be even more imminent when the nonpublic schools were Catholic parochial schools, if there is truth in the accusation cited by George Madaus and Roger Linnan. They wrote that, "the Catholic Schools have been accused over the years of undermining the social consensus within the country and of producing in their students narrow, rigid, sectarian outlooks" (1973:214).

Since the public and parochial systems of education are central to the present study, it would be well to examine and compare the philosophies and objectives of each. There are some basic differences, in theory and in fact, between the philosophies and objectives of education as proposed and practiced by public and Catholic parochial schools.

It is immediately evident from the literature dealing with the public school education that there is no one commonly accepted philosophy of education. In fact, each school district, and to some extent each individual school, is allowed and encouraged to formulate its own philosophy and objectives. James Johnson, et. al. (1969: 290), even state that "Teachers working within the framework of American democracy select a philosophy of education approach which they personally feel best enables them to work with their pupils."

This freedom of choice has resulted in the acceptance of a wide variety of philosophies, as the authors make apparent.

Each of the educational views considered in the following discussion, particularly Essentialism, Perennialism, Progressivism, and Reconstructionism, is practiced with varying degrees of emphasis in today's schools. With regard to present-day application each of the educational views might be thought of as contemporary (Johnson, et.al., 1969:314).

DeYoung and Wynn add their support to the idea that there is a diversity of philosophies. They list what they call the "major educational philosophies of our time." These are existentialism, life-adjustment education, personal psychological development, essentialism, supernaturalism (identified as the philosophy of church-affiliated schools), progressivism, and reconstructionism (1972:40-44).

Thus, it can be seen that there is no one guiding philosophy found in all public schools, rather there is a multiplicity. There has tended to be a more consistent, centralized statement of objectives which have been identified for public school education throughout the years.

In 1918, the Commission of Reorganization of Secondary Education of the National Education Association issued a report which contained the seven cardinal principles of public school education. These were: health, command of the fundamental processes, worthy home membership, vocation, citizenship, worthy use of leisure, and ethical character (Ragan and Shepherd, 1971:113-14).

A decade later, the Department of Superintendence of the National Education Association identified four general areas of education which related the individual to (1) his own growth and development, (2) the world of nature; (3) the systems of organized society; and (4) the Power that in some way orders the development of man and his universe (Ragan and Shepherd, 1971:114-15).

Then in 1938 the Educational Policies Commission of the National Education Association proposed and identified four aspects of educational objectives. These are (1) the objectives of self-realization, (2) the objective of human relationships, (3) the objectives of economic efficiency, and (4) the objectives of civic responsibility. Commenting on these objectives Ragan and Shepherd write:

> This statement of educational objectives recognizes the function of
> education as not only to produce better informed citizens but to
> change their behavior in relation to important individual and social
> problems. It is significant that the "fundamental processes" are
> included under the objectives of self-realization. This reflects the
> modern concept that these subjects are not ends in themselves but
> means to the complete development of the child. If the values implied in this statement of objectives can be implemented in school
> programs all over the nation, the public school will take its place
> as the bulwark of a democratic society (1971:117).

Another study of the objectives of elementary public education was made by the Mid-Century Committee on Outcomes in Elementary Education in 1953. The following areas were identified: physical development, health, body care; individual, social and emotional development; ethical behavior, standards, values; social relation; the social world; the physical world; esthetic development; communication; and quantitative relationships. Appropriate results are listed and evaluated in terms of knowledge and understanding; skills and competencies; attitudes and interests; and action patterns.

> This report assumes that education is for the purpose of bringing
> about desirable changes in behavior, that growth and learning are
> continuous, and that outcomes are to be considered in terms of
> the range of abilities found within a group of children at any of
> the three levels (Ragan and Shepherd, 1971:117).

9

The Educational Policies Commission proclaimed, in 1962, that "The purpose which runs through and strengthens all other purposes--the common thread of education-- is the development of the ability to think" (1962:12). The Commission stated that while rational powers are not all of life or all of mind, and recognized the validity of other traditional objectives, it also pointed out that the development of rational powers provides a solid basis for competence in all the areas with which the school has traditionally been concerned (Ragan and Shepherd, 1971:117-18).

Finally, the President's Science Advisory Committee in 1964, presented its view as to the central purpose or objective of education, which appeared to concur with that previously stated by the Commission. The report stated:

Good education fosters disinterested curiosity and love of understanding, but it also fosters the desire to connect--to connect theory and practice, intelligence and conduct. The Panel believes that today's children must be prepared to cope with new patterns of life, that they must be equipped with good information and trained in viable modes of thinking to create new solutions.

It appears that there is more agreement on a common underlying philosophy found among Catholic parochial schools. This is undoubtedly due in large part to the centralized authority and the common theology accepted by all schools. The Church's official statement on the philosophy of a Catholic education was formulated by Pope Pius XI.

It is therefore as important to make no mistake in education, as it is to make no mistake in the pursuit of the last end, with which the whole work of education is intimately and necessarily connected. In fact, since education consists essentially in preparing man for which he must be and for what he must do here below, that he may attain the sublime end for which he was created, it is clear that we can have no true education which is not wholly directed to man's end. . . (Husslein, 1942: 90-91).

Later in the same document the following objectives are given:

The proper and immediate end of Christian education is to cooperate with divine grace in forming the true and perfect Christian, that is, to form Christ Himself in those regenerated by baptism. . .

For precisely this reason, Christian education takes in the whole aggregate of human life, physical and spiritual, intellectual and moral, individual, domestic and social, not with a view of reducing it in any way, but in order to elevate, regulate, and perfect it, in accordance with the example and teaching of Christ.

Hence the true Christian, product of Christian education, is the supernatural man who thinks, judges, and acts constantly and consistently in accordance with right reason illumined by the supernatural light of the example and teaching of Christ. . . .(1942:118-19).

Commenting on the Catholic philosophy of education, William McGucken wrote:

Scholastic philosophy is theocentric. Catholic life and thought and education have God as their basis. . . . This cornerstone of scholasticism is apt to prove irritating to the modern secularist who either ignores God or relegates Him to lower case. Secularism and naturalism, so characteristic of many American philosophies of education, make it exceedingly difficult for the modern mind trained in these philosophies to understand the Catholic position on this important matter (n.d.:3).

John Redden and Francis Ryan (1956:531) discussed the objectives of a Catholic education.

> Democratic principles have their source in the worth of the individual. The promotion and perpetuation of this ideal is a fundamental secondary objective of the educative process.

> The term secondary objective implies that the educative process has a primary, a more important objective. That primary objective is the attainment of the end for which God created each individual. When, therefore, one speaks of education for democracy and democratic living as an objective of education, it is clear, according to Catholic philosophy, that such objective must be subordinate to, and contributory toward, the fulfillment of man's last end.

A comparison of the two school systems has been made by others in the past. A non-Catholic writer, Howard Mumford Jones, in a lecture at the University of Chicago, stated:

> Let us contrast the Catholic and the non-Catholic traditions in liberal education. Roughly speaking, the problem of values does not arise in the Catholic educational tradition, or if it does arise, it does not arise in the same way. The Catholic university may be objective in matters of pure science, but in the humanities it is not unpartisan and it does not try to be. The core of the Catholic system is theology; theology in turn conditions Catholic ethics and Catholic philosophy; and the Catholic point of view in the interpretation of history and literature is unmistakable. Indeed, it is precisely because the church does not desire to intrust the question of values to irreligious hands that Catholic institutions of higher learning exist. There is a definite point of view which, if it avoids dogma, implies doctrine; and consequently Catholic education in the humanities has a certainty with which one may quarrel, but which in contrast to the confusion of mine among non-Catholic professional educational leaders is admirable (Gray, 1934).

It appears, therefore, that the principle differences between a public education and a Catholic education include the teaching of religion, theology and morality which are central to parochial school education; the Catholic interpretation given to all subject matter which is open to interpretation, as opposed to a more individual and secular interpretation given in the public schools; and the overall agreement and adherence to a common philosophy and set of objectives found in parochial schools as opposed to the multiplicity of philosophies and objectives which are adopted by public schools.

Hypotheses

This section presents a concise statement of the eight specific null hypotheses which were tested in the research. The basic goal referent of these hypotheses was that presented by Milton Gordon of adaptation to the core society and culture; namely, Anglo conformity.

1. There is no difference in the degree of overall assimilation between

eighth grade Mexican Americans in public schools and those in parochial schools.

2. There is no difference in the degree of acculturation between Mexican Americans in the eighth grade in public schools and those in parochial schools

3. There is no difference in the degree of structural assimilation between eighth grade Mexican Americans in public schools and those in parochial schools.

4. There is no difference in the attitude toward amalgamation between Mexican Americans in the eighth grade in public schools and those in parochial schools.

5. There is no difference in the degree of identificational assimilation between eighth grade Mexican Americans in public schools and those in parochial school.

6. There is no difference between attitude receptional assimilation (absence of prejudice) of eighth grade Mexican Americans in public schools and those in parochial schools.

7. There is no difference between behavior receptional assimilation (absence of discrimination) of eighth grade Mexican Americans in public schools and those in parochial schools.

8. There is no difference in the degree of civic assimilation between the eighth grade Mexican Americans in the public schools and those in parochial schools.

CHAPTER II

REVIEW OF THE LITERATURE

Related Research

It was not at all clear, based on the reported findings of previous research, whether one could expect to find a high degree of assimilation among the Mexican Americans. Statements such as the following made it appear that very little assimilation--and hence great differences between Anglo and Mexican American responses--would be found.

This minority group poses a particularly interesting and important area of investigation because, unlike most other ethnic minority groups, it has demonstrated a great deal of apparent resistance to assimilation into the mainstream of modern society; although many Mexican Americans have resided in the United States for three generations or more, they have had a tendency to maintain the patterns of their culture of origin relative to language, religion, family, values, aesthetics, etc. (Kuvlesky and Patella, 1971:231-44).

In two studies of this ethnic group, however, the senior author of the article found almost no significant differences between the occupational and educational expectations, and intensity of aspirations between Mexican American and Anglo respondents (Kuvlesky and Patella, 1971; Kuvlesky, Wright and Juarez, 1971).

There has been some research which is more immediately relevant to the present study, not only because much of it is related to San Antonio but because it is more directly related to the problem being considered in this research project. After presenting the results of several studies and interviews, Moore (1970:88) wrote:

Except perhaps in San Antonio, the ruling spirits of the Roman Catholic Church have been reluctant to take the ideological lead in any of the important issues of past or present for Mexican Americans. . . They viewed assimilation into American life as desirable, but their unwillingness to push assimilation unless Catholicism was also maintained makes it unlikely that they could ever have been a very effective force.

A relatively recent study of Los Angeles revealed that over one-third of the Mexican American children enrolled in secondary schools drop out before completion. Most of them, however, both want and expect some formal education after high school. It was also found that there are some noticeable differences between Mexican American and Anglo students, but these tend to gradually diminish as they progress through school. In fact, these differences are so greatly reduced that by the time the student has gone through the public school system and reached the twelfth grade there is very little difference between the two groups in values and expectations (Moore, 1970:83-84).

In San Antonio the median number of years of schooling completed by persons twenty-five years of age and over was 4.5 for people with Spanish surnames in 1950, as compared to 9.1 years for the total population. There was a slight change shown in the 1960 census, indicating that the median years of formal education for people with a Spanish surname was 5.7 while that of the total population was 10.0. The corresponding figures for Anglos and nonwhites were 12.1 years and 9.4 years respectively (Moore:1970: 68).

Most Mexican Americans who are asked what they want to be called by Anglos usually do not prefer "American." The majority of the people interviewed in recent surveys in Los Angeles, San Antonio and Albuquerque wanted to be called "Mexican American", "Spanish American", or "Latin American". In short, they see themselves as a distinctive people, rather than as one fully merged with an all-encompassing American identity. In 1965-1966, Mexican Americans in San Antonio most often wanted to be called "Latin Americans" (Moore, 1970:8). The results of a survey conducted in the Southwest and published in the San Antonio Light last year revealed that the majority of those interviewed preferred to be called "Mexicano", with the second highest percentage opting for "Mexican American".

Evidence indicates that Mexican Americans do tend to agree with certain features of the Anglo stereotype of them. More than 80 percent of those interviewed in San Antonio and Los Angeles felt that Mexicans are more emotional than other Americans. More than two-thirds felt that they are less progressive than Anglos and that they have stronger family attachments. Over half agreed that Mexican Americans are less materialistic than Anglos. Also ninety-five percent of the Mexican Americans questioned in San Antonio said there was discrimination from the Anglo community (Moore, 1970:8).

Other data collected in San Antonio indicate that low income respondents hold more familistic values than those of medium income, and also are more generally traditional Mexican in their values including their time orientation. Results from studies reveal that in San Antonio, as in other parts of the country, the clanishness of the Mexican American is lessening from generation to generation so that whereas 70 percent of the adult respondents reported having limited their primary relations in their childhood to those of their own ethnic group, only 39 percent of them stated that their childrens' friends were limited to other Mexican Americans (Moore, 1970:129-35).

In Moore's book Mexican Americans a table for the year 1965-1966 is presented showing the percent of Mexican American respondents in San Antonio who live in an ethnic neighborhood (colony) versus those who live outside of it (frontier), having predominantly or all Anglo associates. The figures reveal that those in the colony are much more likely to use other Mexican Americans as both a membership group and as a reference group. On the other hand, those in the frontier are more likely to use Anglos (1970:111-12).

In the same source it is shown that in San Antonio for the years 1940-1955, approximately 90 percent of the Mexican Americans married within their own group (1970: 115). It was pointed out, however, that with each succeeding generation the rate of exogamous marriages tended to increase. A much more recent study of Los Angeles County found that

> the data indicate that marriage of second and third-generation
> Mexican Americans are assimilationists. Both men and women are
> more likely to marry 'Anglo' than to marry immigrants from Mexico.
> Among third-generation persons, the chances are actually higher
> that he or she will marry an Anglo than either a first- or second-
> generation Mexican (Mittlebach and Moore, 1968:54).

When writing the implications of the above cited study, the authors state:

> We feel that our findings strongly suggest the assimilative potential
> of the population when external barriers are comparatively low,
> though this potential has been generally depreciated (1968:61).

The study, then, indicates that ethnic outmarriage, or exogamy, tends to increase with each succeeding generation, and also with a rise in socio-economic status. It is interesting to note, in this regard, that intermarriage has been considered by some to be the ultimate proof of assimilation.

Finally, surveys show that most Mexican Americans in the cities of Los Angeles, San Antonio, and Albuquerque are bilingual in English and Spanish, although there are some who speak only English or Spanish. Most of those who speak Spanish in Los Angeles and San Antonio were either Mexican-born or have Mexican-born parents (Moore, 1970:120). The importance of language, especially the use of Spanish among peers, has been reported in several studies. Generally speaking, the greater or more frequent the use of Spanish, the stronger is the identification with, and participation in, the Mexican American subculture (Nall, 1962; Penalosa and McDonagh, 1966).

Related Theory

A review of the literature revealed several theories which attempt to explain differential rates of assimilation, and although they were not specifically formulated to explain the Mexican American situation, they are readily applicable. Those which were felt to have particular relevancy are presented, along with a brief statement which will indicate how they apply to the situation under investigation.

Warner and Srole, drawing on the results of many researches involving various minorities, specify the factors which affect the speed with which minority groups can attain assimilation in the United States. They also present a "scale of subordination and assimilation" which is based on the variables of cultural and biological traits. After applying their scales to the case of the Mexican American--who are classified as Cultural Type 4 (Catholics and other non-Protestants who do not speak English) and Racial Type 3 (Mongoloid and Caucasoid mixture) they arrived at the conclusion:

> These Catholics, most of them darkskinned Latin Americans, are heavily subordinated as compared with moderate and light subordination for the same type in the other two racial categories. The prediction for their assimilation is slow, which is to say there is no predictable time when they will disappear into the total population, whereas that of their co-religionists of lighter skin is predicted to be short and moderate (1945:295).

Later they speculate on the future of these groups:

> These ethno-racial groups are likely to divide into two parts: If and when the Spanish Americans and Mexicans lose their cultural identity, those of the more Caucasoid type will become a part of our class order and be capable of rising in our social hierarchy. The darker ones will probably become semicasts. There is some evidence that it may be possible that this latter group will merge with the Mongoloid or Negroid groups (1945:295).

In a paper whose stated purpose was to consider the adequacy of the Warner-Srole scheme in the light of recently gathered data in the Southwest, the authors concluded that given certain conditions which have been occurring since 1940, "one can hypothesize that the rate of mobility and assimilation will increase rapidly in the next generation" (D'Antonio and Samora, 1962:24).

An earlier proposition of Warner and Srole which is also applicable to the Mexican American is that the greater the proximity and access to the homeland, the slower the rate of assimilation (1945:100-01). Proximity makes it relatively easy for immigrants to return to their original homeland, i.e., to Mexico, for periodic visits or have their friends and relatives visit them. These visits may enable the immigrant to avoid deeply rooted ties and commitments within the new homeland. It also enables them to experience a periodic reinforcement of their original cultural traditions and life patterns. This undoubtedly applies to some degree to the Mexican Americans who live in San Antonio, which lays approximately 150 miles from the border.

Robin M. Williams, Jr. proposes that the larger the ratio of the incoming group to the resident population, or the more rapid the influx of the incoming group, the slower the rate of assimilation (1947:58). If the influx of immigrants is too great or too rapid, the native population tends to view them as a threat and begins to erect various segregating barriers. There is no way to know what the actual influx of Mexicans into San Antonio is because, being located near one of the major ports of entry, Laredo, large numbers of immigrants and visitors, both legal and illegal, pass through. According to the last census, slightly over half of the population (52%) is classified as Mexican American, based on a Spanish surname. However, Mexicans or Mexican Americans have been residents as long as the Anglos, and are not then really an incoming group in the complete sense of the word.

Due largely to the military bases which are located in the area, it is a city with a very mobile and transient population, and hence the more stable element of the city is accustomed to seeing, and dealing with newcomers. This situation makes any influx in the Mexican American community relatively unnoticeable in this large city.

Schermerhorn alerts us to the proposition that the greater the dispersion of the group, especially in the same territorial pattern as the dominant group, the more rapid will be its assimilation (1949:460). Where immigrant groups are concentrated in large numbers, such as ghettos or barrios, they tend to perpetuate their native cultures. On the other hand, there they are scattered they are less capable of preserving their identity and different culture. In San Antonio, while the west side is predominately Mexican American, there are so many that they are found in virtually all parts of the city.

Alexander Weinstock offers the hypotheses that the higher the educational, income, and occupational levels of the incoming group, the more rapid its assimilation (1964:321-40). In general, height on the scale is correlated with increases in the number and importance of peripheral role elements which effect the acculturation rate by intensifying pressures to accept social patterns of the new society. Also, class prejudice or acceptance enters here, the lower the class of the newcomer the less desirable he is in general. Most of the Mexican Americans in Southwest Texas are from rural lower class backgrounds, although many who live in San Antonio are generations removed from this background.

Finally, Stanley Lieberson states that for the most part, subordinate migrants appear to be more rapidly assimilated than are subordinate idigenous populations. Also, the former are generally under greater pressures to assimilate than are the latter (1961:902-10). There are more psychological and social pressures and motivations for an immigrant group to adapt to the established culture and society of the newly chosen homeland. These same pressures and motives are not as strong or compelling for an indigenous people to change for an incoming group. In Texas, as in many of the southwestern states, Mexicans were more of an indigenous people than the Anglos who took over the territory which was ceded to the United States after the Mexican-American War in 1848. However, it is doubtful that many of the Mexican Americans can trace their residency back so far. Most are probably in San Antonio due to the large numbers of immigrants who entered from Mexico during and after World War I--when almost one million entered between 1910 and 1930 (Rose, 1964:42-43)--and World War II when many Mexicans filled the vacancies created by the draft. Others are more recent arrivals having come as "Wetbacks" who crossed the border illegally or "Braceros" who entered legally as contract laborers.

CHAPTER III

THE RESEARCH DESIGN

The Instrument

In order to test the hypotheses stated in Chapter One, it was necessary to measure the various aspects of assimilation which were indicated by Gordon. The instrument was divided into seven separate sections with each of the sections designed to test a different subtype of assimilation, and hence a different hypothesis. The following indicates the section of the questionnaire, the subtype of assimilation with which it treats and the specific hypothesis which it tests:

Section I	acculturation	hypothesis 2
Section II	civic assimilation	hypothesis 8
Section III	identificational assimilation	hypothesis 5
Section IV	behavior receptional assimilation	hypothesis 7
Section V	attitude receptional assimilation	hypothesis 6
Section VI	(attitude toward) amalgamation	hypothesis 4
Section VII	structural assimilation	hypothesis 3

The total score of all the sections indicates the overall degree of assimilation and therefore tests hypothesis 1. In general, there is a direct relationship between score and assimilation. For each section, as for the test as a whole, a higher score indicates greater assimilation of the respondent. Because of the youth of the respondents it was the attitude and tendency toward amalgamation (hypothesis 4) rather than the actual degree of amalgamation which was measured.

The questionnaire was composed of different types of questions to elicit the necessary information. In all cases the instrument was designed not only to give the desired data, but to require a minimum of time and effort in answering. Therefore most questions took the form of forced-choice replies with the respondent indicating his response by circling the proper choice. This not only facilitated the scoring procedure, but also insured that the necessary information was obtained.

In all sections except the last one, attitudes were determined by means of statements to which the contestants responded on a Likert-type scale. Responses were arranged along a five-point scale from strongly agree to undecided to strongly disagree, so that varying degrees of acceptance or rejection, intensity of response, and gradation of belief would be reflected. Section V included questions which required the respondent to rank in order of preference the choices which were presented. Sections VI and VII had questions which directed the respondent to list the names of friends or organizations, according to the instructions of each specific item.

The selection of items was carefully undertaken. A review of the literature was made to determine items for possible inclusion on this test. Selection was made on the basis of two principle criteria: first, the relevance to the particular aspects of assimilation being tested, and second, the possibility of differentiating between an ideal or typical Mexican attitude and a corresponding American Anglo attitude.

Items thus chosen were grouped into sections according to the seven subtypes of assimilation. All items included in a given section were considered to measure the same aspect of assimilation. The resulting list of statements was then shown to a group of college professors whom the researcher felt were able to aid with their comments and criticism. All consultants had earned the Doctor of Philosophy degree, these included: four sociologists, two psychologists, one educator, one philosopher, and one political scientist. Those statements which were chosen were incorporated in the instrument which was then presented to the eighth grade of a parochial school. Students on the pretest were given the same instructions which were later used in the actual administration of the questionnaire. They were, however, encouraged to ask questions and were instructed to leave blank those questions which they did not understand, and to underline the words or phrases which caused them trouble. Statements which were ambiguous or difficult to understand were deleted or reworded.

The revised questionnaire was composed of 78 items, including 4 which were needed to establish the ethnic group, religion, and school system of the respondents. This instrument was administered to over 500 eighth-grade students, including 388 Mexican Americans and 78 Anglos, in 20 different schools in San Antonio. Half of these schools were public schools randomly selected, while the other half were parochial schools which were specially chosen because of their close physical proximity to each of the public schools. These public schools represented 3 different school districts, and although there was no deliberate attempt to obtain a wide geographic representation, the resulting distribution of the schools which were selected found all parts of the city represented. Two of the schools are located in the north of San Antonio, two in the east, three in the southern part of the city, two in the west, and one in the northwest.

Rather than pick the parochial schools randomly, it was felt that it would be preferable to select them on the basis of proximity to the randomly-selected public schools. This, it was felt, would provide some measure of control over possible relevant variables which might be related to the physical location of the schools.

The actual location of each of the ten public schools to be used was marked on a map of the city, then with the aid of a directory listing all parochial schools, and a member of the Archdiocesan Chancery Office of San Antonio and several parochial school principals, the researcher was able to locate the ten closest coeducational parochial schools.

Selection of the students took the form of a systematic sample as described in the literature (Selltiz, et.al., 1967:523). Twenty-eight names were picked from the alphabetically ordered class lists at each of the schools. In several of the parochial schools the entire eighth grade class was used because it was only slightly larger than the desired sample size. Results of the data obtained were statistically analyzed and revealed that the instrument was capable of discriminating between Mexican American and Anglo students as well as public and parochial school students.

Finally, it was felt that the instrument should be standardized on some groups outside of San Antonio and the South Texas area because of the pervasive Mexican and Catholic influences which may have affected the Anglo respondents. The neighboring state of Louisiana was selected, where the Mexican influence is virtually nonexistant and the Catholic influence rather weak. Sixty teenage white Anglo Protestants from in and around Baton Rouge were given the questionnaire. Almost all of them were either Baptist or Methodists. The questionnaire was also given to thirty teenage Latin Americans residing in Baton Rouge and New Orleans who had been in the United States for no more than a year or two. This was done to insure that they were not yet "Americanized", so that their responses to the items would reflect the Latin American culture. In order to facilitate this, the questionnaire was also translated into Spanish. After the researcher had translated all the items, a copy of the English and Spanish translations was given to three native Spanish speakers each from different countries who were asked to make any necessary corrections. The final translated instrument was given to those who could not read English sufficiently well to answer it in English. In all, only seven persons utilized the Spanish translation. It was found that there were no significant differences between the answers of the Latin Americans who answered in

English and those who answered in Spanish.

Each of the item responses of the Anglo Protestants and the Latin Americans were then compared by means of Student's t. Those items which did not meet the 1.75 level which is recommended for this item selection procedure by Edwards (1957:153) were eliminated from the final instrument. In all, only eight items were found to lack the necessary discriminatory power, and were thus eliminated. See Appendix A for the t values on each of the items.

After the final item selection was made, which resulted in the adoption of sixty-six items relating to assimilation, fourteen additional questions were added to obtain personal information about the respondent. This information felt to be relevant to the study, which was thus obtained, was used as test factors as recommended by Rosenberg (1968), when the item data were analyzed. This personal data included questions to determine the school system, sex, ethnic background, religion and socio-economic status (SES) of the respondent. In addition, there were five questions which combined to give a "religiosity" score (RS), and three questions which together yielded an "aspirational level" score (AL). The final questions determined if the respondent had ever attended the other school system, i.e., had parochial school students ever attended public schools, and vice versa, and if so, the total number of years in attendance. Average time required to complete the entire questionnaire was thirty minutes. See Appendix B for a copy of the final instrument.

Scoring

All items which were of the Likert-type were scored in the same way. After reading each statement the respondent selected one of the five options indicating his personal feeling toward the attitude object. A five point rating scale was employed to assign values to each option: strongly agree = 5 or 1; agree = 4 or 2; undecided = 3; disagree = 2 or 4; strongly disagree = 1 or 5. The assignment of maximum or minimum values 5 or 1 depended on the particular statement and the way it was answered by the Anglo respondents. Since the objective of this research was to ascertain the degree of assimilation of Mexican Americans into our WASP society, the "correct" answer, for scoring purposes, was that which the majority of the white Anglo Protestants in Baton Rouge chose, but only in terms of the general agreement or disagreement. Therefore, it was the direction of the Anglo response, rather than the intensity, which was taken into consideration when scoring was done. In all cases 5 represented the highest possible score and degree of assimilation, and 1 represented the lowest possible score and, hence, least degree of assimilation.

In the scoring of those items (number 1 and 4, Section V) which required the respondent to rank the various ethnic groups 1 through 5, in order of preference and inferiority respectively, only the ranking given to Anglos was considered relevant and scored. If a Mexican American respondent ranked the Anglo as his first preference then a 5 was given, if ranked as his second preference then a 4 was given, and so on until a last place preference was assigned the value of 1. When ranking according to inferiority a first place choice was given a 1, a second place choice was given a 2, a third place choice a 3, etc. Since most Mexican American are Catholic--93.2 percent of the sample and an almost identical percentage nationwide (Moore, 1970:84-85)--and our Anglo society is basically Protestant, the scoring on the item (number 2, Section V) dealing with religion was based on how the Catholics ranked the Protestants, as with the ethnic group items, and vice versa.

On item 3, Section V, where ethnic-group membership was combined with religious membership, both variables were taken into consideration in the scoring. Thus, the score was based on the rank given to a Protestant Anglo (or Catholic Anglo) by a

Catholic Mexican American (or Protestant Mexican American). A value of 5 was, therefore, assigned to a Catholic Mexican American who gave top preference to a Protestant Anglo, or a Protestant Mexican American who gave preference to a Catholic Anglo. Since there were eight possible choices instead of the customary five, some adjustment was made in the scoring procedure when dealing with anything other than a first or last-place choice. The adjustment was made as follows: first-choice = 5, second- or third-choice = 4, fourth- or fifth-choice = 3, sixth- or seventh-choice = 2, and the last-choice = 1 point.

A similar but slightly different procedure was used in scoring the items (numbers 1, 2, 3, Section VI, and numbers 1, 2, 3, Section VII) which required the respondent to list the last names of friends and dates. As with the previous scoring procedure, scoring was based on Mexican Americans including Anglo surnames. The score was based on the percentage of Anglo surnames which appeared in the list of a Mexican American respondent. When three of the five surnames were Anglo, then the score was 3/5 of 5. Five, which was the maximum assimilation score, served as the basis for all computations. In the above case the resulting score was 3. In those cases where the respondent listed less than the five names which were provided for in the questionnaire, the scoring procedure was the same but usually resulted in a fraction rather than a whole number. Thus, one Anglo surname in a list of three names resulted in 1/3 of 5 or a score of 1.66 which when rounded off was scored as 1.7. When no names were listed and the respondent entered the word "none" according to prior instructions, the minimum score of 1 was assigned.

In order to assign a score to number 4, Section VII, it was necessary to take into consideration the answers on the following item, number 5, which was not scored separately. The combined treatment of both together resulted in a procedure which was utilized on the preceeding items. The rationale for this was that those clubs, teams, groups or associations which appeared in number 4 but not in number 5 were structurally assimilated. Therefore, when four groups, clubs, teams, or associations were listed in number 4 and two of them were also listed in item number 5, then the score assigned was 2/4 of 5 or 2.5. If all of the clubs, teams, groups or associations were integrated or assimilated (as indicated by being listed in number 4 but not in number 5), regardless of how many there were, a score of 5 was given. When a respondent belonged to no clubs, teams, groups or associations, or only belonged to non-integrated or assimilated ones (number 5), a score of 1 was assigned.

On all items in the questionnaire the scores ranged from a maximum of 5 points to a minimum of 1 point. The maximum and minimum scores by sections are listed in Table 1 as follows:

TABLE 1

POSSIBLE MAXIMUM AND MINIMUM SCORES BY SECTION

SECTION	MAXIMUM SCORE	MINIMUM SCORE
I	80	16
II	60	12
III	55	11
IV	40	8
V	40	8
VI	35	7
VII	20	4
TOTALS	330	66

Validity

It has been stated by Mouly (1963:252) that:

at the most elementary level, it is necessary for the questionnaire
to have face validity--that is, each question must be related to
the topic under investigation, there must be an adequate coverage
of the overall topic, the questions must be clear and unambiguous,
and so on.

Because of the means used in the selection of the items which were included in the instrument, and the review of each item by the researcher and consulting experts previously
mentioned, as well as the extensive pretest, it was felt that the face validity of the
instrument was insured.

Unfortunately, it was not possible to check the validity of the instrument by
comparison to some external criterion, as is recommended. The researcher has not been
able to find such an external criterion, therefore this type of validation is lacking.
As an accepted alternative (Kerlinger, 1964:454), however, known groups, namely WASP and
Latin American, were given the questionnaire, and their answers differed significantly
and in the expected manner or direction.

The Sample

The population to be tested was limited to eighth grade Mexican American students within the San Antonio city limits (excluding those schools which are located on
military installations for dependent children) attending either public or parochial coeducational institutions. Due to the high drop out rate among Mexican Americans in
high schools (NEA, 1970:107), it was felt that it was best to limit the respondents to
the eighth grade, before they reach their sixteenth birthday, at which time they could
legally leave school. After sixteen the sample tends to be more skewed in favor of
those who are more assimilated, since those who drop out appear to be those who could
not or would not adjust to the Anglo way. Prior studies have indicated that most drop-
outs leave school sometime between the ages of 16 and 17 years, usually just before,
during, or immediately following the ninth grade (Wolfbien, 1959; Tesseneer and
Tesseneer, 1958; U.S. Dept. of Labor, 1960).

The respondents were male and female, Mexican American (non-whites were excluded) students currently enrolled in one of the selected institutions. The 1971-1972
Public School Directory, published by the Texas Education Agency, was consulted to
determine which public schools were in San Antonio, and to obtain the names, addresses
and school districts to which they belong (1971:8-12). In all there were thirty-eight
eligible public schools.

It was decided that the sample would be drawn from eighteen schools, of which
nine would be in the public school system and nine in the parochial school system. Of
these nine schools, in each of the respective systems, an attempt was made to get three
low, three medium, and three high in SES, as measured by the father's occupation of the
eighth grade respondents. Data obtained from the previous test of the twenty schools
was used as the basis for this determination and selection. In those few cases where
it was necessary to pick a school not previously studied, because of insufficient number
of the necessary SES types, the selection of an unknown school was made only after consulting knowledgeable educators and administrators regarding their probable SES standing.
The nine public schools thus selected represented four independent school districts.
The districts to which they belong are listed as follows:

Edgewood Independent School District

    Brentwood Junior High School
    Truman Junior High School
    Escobar Junior High School

Harlandale Independent School District

    Harlandale Middle School
    Southcross Middle School
    Terrell Wells Middle School

Judson Independent School District

    Kirby Junior High School

South San Antonio Independent School District

    Alan Shepard Middle School
    Dwight Junior High School

The following are the nine parochial schools which were chosen:

    St. Teresa's Academy
    St. Patrick's School
    St. Philip of Jesus School
    St. Gerard's School
    St. Ann's School
    St. Paul's School
    Guadalupe School
    St. Joseph School
    St. Leo's School

It was decided that a suitable sample size could be obtained by administering the questionnaire to one whole class from each of the eighteen schools. This would result in a possible sample of some 400 students since most schools in the area have classes which range from 25-35 students. Due to the high percentage of Mexican Americans in the population of San Antonio, particularly in the school districts selected, it was virtually assured that sufficient ethnically eligible students would be included to achieve a satisfactory sample size (U.S. Commission on Civil Rights, 1971: 24-25).

Following the previously stated definition for Mexican Americans, anyone who had at least one Black parent was considered Black or one Oriental parent was therefore Oriental and thus his or her questionnaire was eliminated from the final analysis although in order to avoid the embarrassment of discrimination they were allowed to answer. In all, there were 140 completed questionnaires which were discarded because of Black, Oriental or Anglo parentage. Of these, 112 were Anglo, two were Mexican American-Black, two were Mexican American-Oriental, five were Oriental-Oriental, and four were Anglo-Oriental. The remaining fifteen were Black-Black. Refer to Tables 2 and 3, respectively, to see the total size of the class, and the corresponding usable sample sizes for each public and parochial school.

After the eighteen schools were selected and permission obtained from the necessary authority in each case, the researcher arranged a date to meet the class of students. In almost all parochial schools there was only one eighth grade class, while in most public schools there were between 10-15 eighth grade classes. Placement of students in these classes, however, was more or less random, as no effort was made to group according to any social, physical or educational characteristics. Every class was felt to be representative of the population of the particular school. Therefore, there should be no systematic bias in the sampling procedure due to utilization of entire classes.

After the students were selected, a time and place was arranged at each of the respective schools. Usually the actual administration of the instrument took place a week after the arrangements were made. In all it took approximately four months to complete the gathering of the required information.

TABLE 2

PUBLIC SCHOOL, NUMBER TESTED*, NUMBER INCLUDED IN TOTAL SAMPLE,
AND PERCENTAGE CONTRIBUTED TO TOTAL PUBLIC SCHOOL SAMPLE

School	No. Tested	No. in Sample	Percent of Sample
Southcross	28	28	16.67
Harlandale	32	23	13.69
Terrell Wells	31	20	11.90
Brentwood	31	25	14.88
Truman	29	28	16.67
Dwight	29	18	10.71
Escobar	16	15	8.93
Alan Shepard	29	8	4.76
Kirby	29	3	1.79
TOTALS	254	168	100.00

*It was necessary to administer the questionnaire to all students present in class even though they were ethnically ineligible for inclusion in the sample tested.

TABLE 3

PAROCHIAL SCHOOL, NUMBER TESTED*, NUMBER INCLUDED IN TOTAL SAMPLE,
AND PERCENTAGE CONTRIBUTED TO TOTAL PAROCHIAL SCHOOL SAMPLE

School	No. Tested	No. in Sample	Percent of Sample
St. Ann	35	29	13.49
St. Patrick	32	23	10.70
St. Leo	19	17	7.91
St. Paul	31	25	11.63
St. Teresa	33	26	12.08
St. Joseph	22	15	6.98
Guadalupe	30	30	13.95
St. Gerard	32	17	7.91
St. Philip	35	33	15.35
TOTALS	269	215	100.00

*It was necessary to administer the questionnaire to all students present in class even though they were ethnically ineligible for inclusion in the sample tested.

At the prearranged time and place--usually an empty classroom--the researcher met with the students and explained what was expected of them. In order to avoid any possible "Hawthorne effect" on the part of the Mexican Americans by telling them the true nature of the research, the students were merely told that they were taking part in a study which was interested in finding out the attitudes and feelings of all eighth grade students in San Antonio on a wide variety of issues. It was pointed out to them that no identification of the respondents was either desired or possible, and the necessity of answering truthfully was stressed. This explanation was read to them in a prepared statement, a copy of which appears in the Appendix. See Appendix C.

Next, the instructions which appear on the instrument were read and explained to them, and the students were told that if anyone did not know the meaning of a word or had any other question after they started to answer, they were to raise their hand and the researcher would answer their questions on an individual basis. Relatively few questions were asked.

According to prior instructions, each respondent turned in his completed questionnaire as he finished. This allowed the researcher time to look over each of the items to make certain that every one had been answered. When an item was found that had been overlooked or otherwise unanswered, the questionnaire was returned to the respondent for completion. In this way incomplete questionnaires were avoided.

The final total number responding was 523, of whom 254 (48.6 percent) were from public schools and 269 (51.4 percent) from parochial schools. The total number of respondents used to test the hypotheses, 383 (73.2 percent of those who completed the questionnaires) were classified as Mexican Americans. Most of these were from endogamous marriages, 352 (91.9 percent), and the remaining 31 were from exogamous marriages, with 23 (6.0 percent) of these having an Anglo father, and 8 (2.1 percent) an

Anglo mother. See Table 4 for a more complete treatment of the sample composition.

Statistical Techniques

The data were handled in several different ways in order to better understand the results. Taken as a whole, the number and percentage of Mexican American respondents who answered each question in each of the possible ways was calculated, and appear in Table 5.

In order to see if the differences in the responses between Mexican American parochial school students and Mexican American public school students for each of the questions were significant, Student's t was computed. The alpha level was set at .05. In testing the hypotheses, the data were treated both as ordinal level (Selltiz, et.al., 1967:369), and as interval level (Labovitz, 1967).

All eight of the null hypotheses were tested by means of Student's t, which tested the significance of difference between the means of the Mexican American students in public schools and those Mexican American students in parochial schools on each of the particular variables. Each hypothesis was tested while controlling for each of the listed test variables.

In addition to testing the hypotheses by using the data as interval level, they were also tested by means of the Mann-Whitney U test considering the data as ordinal level. This test was used to compare the responses of Public-Parochial, Male-Female, Catholic-Non-Catholic, and Middle-Working class respondents. Further testing was not done because the resulting correlation between the U and t tests on all the above was found to be .939.

TABLE 4

COMPOSITION OF SAMPLE

School System	Sex		Religion		Class					Aspiration		
	M	F	C	NC	M	W	H	M	L	H	M	L
Public	78	90	143	25	29	127	44	84	40	86	70	12
Catholic	110	105	214	1	90	117	77	137	1	145	62	8
TOTALS	188	195	357	26	119	244*	121	221	41	231	132	20

*There were 20 respondents who because of the nature of their responses could not be classified.

25

TABLE 5

RESPONSES OF TOTAL SAMPLE BY SECTION AND ITEM*

Section I	Strongly Agree	Agree	Undecided	Disagree	Strongly Disagree
Item					
1	169(44.1)	162(42.3)	23(6.0)	17(4.4)	12(3.1)
2	20(5.2)	89(23.2)	41(10.7)	128(33.4)	105(27.4)
3	68(17.8)	134(35.0)	99(25.8)	53(13.8)	29(7.6)
4	154(40.2)	172(44.9)	26(6.8)	18(4.7)	13(3.4)
5	27(7.0)	104(27.2)	70(18.3)	135(35.2)	47(12.3)
6	42(11.0)	88(23.0)	53(13.8)	119(31.1)	80(20.9)
7	80(20.9)	149(38.9)	77(20.1)	46(12.0)	30(7.8)
8	203(53.0)	152(39.7)	11(2.9)	10(2.6)	6(1.6)
9	64(16.7)	73(19.1)	79(20.6)	113(29.5)	53(13.8)
10	30(7.8)	77(20.1)	111(29.0)	118(30.8)	46(12.0)
11	143(37.3)	167(43.6)	38(9.9)	21(5.5)	13(3.4)
12	29(7.6)	95(24.8)	59(15.4)	127(33.2)	72(18.8)
13	109(28.5)	120(31.3)	52(13.6)	77(20.1)	24(6.3)
14	27(7.0)	160(41.8)	83(21.7)	91(23.8)	22(5.7)
15	37(9.7)	107(27.9)	107(27.9)	89(23.2)	43(11.2)
16	28(7.3)	64(16.7)	45(11.7)	118(30.8)	128(33.4)

Section II					
Item					
1	31(8.1)	59(15.4)	60(15.7)	122(31.9)	110(28.7)
2	8(2.1)	36(9.4)	54(14.1)	189(49.3)	95(24.8)
3	53(13.8)	80(20.9)	90(23.5)	117(30.5)	42(11.0)
4	28(7.3)	137(35.8)	100(26.1)	74(19.3)	43(11.2)
5	87(22.7)	116(30.3)	127(33.2)	37(9.7)	15(3.9)
6	14(3.7)	87(22.7)	151(39.4)	88(23.0)	42(11.0)
7	122(31.9)	124(32.4)	85(22.2)	22(5.7)	29(7.6)
8	20(5.2)	49(12.8)	138(36.0)	122(31.9)	53(13.8)
9	133(34.7)	200(52.2)	27(7.0)	17(4.4)	5(1.3)
10	71(18.5)	136(35.5)	74(19.3)	61(15.9)	40(10.4)
11	117(30.5)	174(45.4)	34(8.9)	52(13.6)	5(1.3)
12	255(66.6)	88(23.0)	15(3.9)	10(2.6)	14(3.7)

TABLE 5 - Continued

Section III	Strongly Agree	Agree	Undecided	Disagree	Strongly Disagree
Item					
1	104(27.2)	93(24.3)	68(17.8)	71(18.5)	45(11.7)
2	127(33.2)	168(43.9)	38(9.9)	40(10.4)	8(2.1)
3	154(40.2)	176(46.0)	32(8.4)	15(3.9)	4(1.0)
4	67(17.5)	205(53.5)	89(23.2)	17(4.4)	3(0.8)
5	6(1.6)	39(10.2)	36(9.4)	179(46.7)	121(31.6)
6	25(6.5)	59(15.4)	129(33.7)	113(29.5)	55(14.4)
7	80(20.9)	145(37.9)	83(21.7)	61(15.9)	12(3.1)
8	103(26.9)	211(55.1)	44(11.5)	18(4.7)	5(1.3)
9	47(12.3)	76(19.8)	68(17.8)	131(34.2)	59(15.4)
10	86(22.5)	119(31.1)	53(13.8)	89(23.2)	34(8.9)
11	67(17.5)	125(32.6)	93(24.3)	75(19.6)	21(5.5)
Section IV					
Item					
1	65(17.0)	195(50.9)	47(12.3)	50(13.1)	24(6.3)
2	78(20.4)	172(44.9)	45(11.7)	67(17.5)	19(5.0)
3	69(18.0)	141(36.8)	28(7.3)	98(25.6)	45(11.7)
4	41(10.7)	98(25.6)	94(24.5)	99(25.8)	49(12.8)
5	16(4.2)	43(11.2)	49(12.8)	176(46.0)	97(25.3)
6	76(19.8)	150(39.2)	59(15.4)	72(18.8)	24(6.3)
7	65(17.0)	200(52.2)	53(13.8)	55(14.4)	8(2.1)
8	26(6.8)	95(24.8)	106(27.7)	109(28.5)	45(11.7)
Section V					
Item					
5	14(3.7)	36(9.4)	90(23.5)	137(35.8)	106(27.7)
6	9(2.3)	17(4.4)	33(8.6)	165(43.1)	159(41.5)
7	15(3.9)	12(3.1)	45(11.7)	164(42.8)	147(38.4)
8	12(3.1)	18(4.7)	38(9.9)	109(28.5)	206(53.8)
Section VI					
Item					
4	8(2.1)	44(11.5)	77(20.1)	141(36.8)	113(29.5)
5	44(11.5)	104(27.2)	170(44.4)	43(11.2)	22(5.7)
6	22(5.7)	32(8.4)	232(60.6)	68(17.8)	29(7.6)
7	11(2.9)	16(4.2)	229(59.8)	87(22.7)	38(9.9)

*Because the results do not lend themselves to inclusion in a table
of this kind, items requiring listing or ranking were not included.

Simple F tests, to determine the homogeneity of population, were also computed between Mexican American students in public schools and those in parochial schools for each of the seven different subtypes of assimilation and also for the overall assimilation, which was taken as measured by the total scores.

Finally, correlation coefficients using the Pearson r, were computed between each of the seven sections--each of which measure a separate aspect of assimilation--and also a correlation coefficient between each section and the grand total. Refer to Table 6 on the following for complete results.

TABLE 6

CORRELATION COEFFICIENTS BETWEEN EACH OF THE SECTIONS
AND EACH SECTION AND THE TOTAL

	Section 1	Section 2	Section 3	Section 4	Section 5	Section 6	Section 7	Total
Section 1	1.000							
Section 2	0.383	1.000						
Section 3	0.007	0.277	1.000					
Section 4	0.147	0.262	0.284	1.000				
Section 5	0.364	0.334	0.163	0.280	1.000			
Section 6	0.101	0.172	0.147	0.088	0.124	1.000		
Section 7	0.268	0.232	0.196	0.246	0.327	0.522	1.000	
Total	0.606	0.693	0.522	0.571	0.636	0.430	0.603	1.000

Test Variables

In order to enhance our understanding of the relationship between the various types of assimilation, and attendance at a parochial or public school, other variables were introduced into the analysis. Thus, analysis of the data included holding constant certain associated variables to aid interpretation. This elaboration was done by means of subgroup classification, in which each test factor was stratified.

In addition to controlling for school system and ethnic group, which were integral aspects of the hypotheses to be tested, several other variables were considered to be worthy of inspection because of their possible direct or indirect effects on the assimilation process. These associated variables were:

Sex (male - female).

Religion (Catholic - non-Catholic) On the pretest questionnaire administered to over
    500 students in twenty schools the choices were Catholic, Protestant, Jew,
    and other. No one identified himself as Jew so that category was eliminated
    in the final instrument. In the final coding for the purpose of analysis,
    other and Protestant were combined together in the category non-Catholic.

Occupation (middle class - working class) Based on the occupation of the respondents'
father--even though at the time he may have been dead, retired or unemployed--
the individual was assigned to an SES. This classification was made on the
basis of Hollingshead's classification of occupations as presented by Melvin
Kohn (1969:12-13).[1] In justifying the use of occupation as the sole indicator
of SES he states:

> The correlation of the family's class position, as judged by Holling-
> shead and Myers, to the head of the household's occupational score was
> 0.88, sufficiently high to indicate that the two indices were measur-
> ing much the same thing. . . . Thus, one can conclude that Holling-
> shead's classification of occupations is a good indication of how know-
> ledgeable sociologists, having very complete data at their disposal,
> would judge men's social class position. The occupational classifica-
> tion is as valid (or nearly as valid) as is informed sociological
> judgement (1969:14).

If there was no occupation for the father, the mother's occupation was used
in determining the SES.

Religiosity (high - medium - low) This was comprised of five different questions dealing with religious instruction and practice. The classification of the respondent was high, medium, or low. In order to facilitate the understanding
and presentation of the classification procedure, the responses have been
coded as follows:

Church attendance:		Family prayer:		Bible reading:	
once a week	1	daily	1	daily	1
a month	2	weekly	2	weekly	2
a year	3	infrequently	3	infrequently	3
less often	4	never	4	never	4

High Those students who indicated no more than one 3 or 4 on the above questions, and "yes" for both questions regarding religious instruction and religious training; or, no 3 or 4 on the questions above, and no more than one "no"
on religious instruction and religious training.

Medium Those excluded from the category above and who responded with at least
one 1 or 2 on the above three questions and one "yes" on both the questions of
religious instruction, and training; or, indicated 1 or 2 on the three questions noted above, and "no" to both questions regarding religious instruction
and training.

Low All the rest.

Aspirational Level (high - medium - low). This was arrived at on the basis of three
separate questions, two dealing with college education and one which required
the respondent to indicate the career or occupation he or she would like to
pursue in the future. This latter answer was scored in accordance with the
Hollingshead classification as above. The following were the criteria for
each of the classifications:

High Those students who indicated "yes" on both questions, and selected a
middle class occupation.

Medium Those who answered "yes" to both questions but selected a working class occupation; or "no" to one or both questions but selected a middle class occupation.

Low   Those who indicated "no" to both questions and selected a working class occupation.

School System Attendance Consistency (high - medium - low). The classifications were based on the number of years the respondent had been a student in the school system currently attended, i.e., public or parochial, as a proportion of his or her entire primary school attendance. Thus, a person who had spent at least two-thirds of his or her school career in the same system, regardless of changing schools, was classified as high. A person who spent at least one-third but less than two-thirds of his or her school career in the same system was classified medium, and a person who had spent less than one-third of his or her career in the same school system was classified as low.

Ethnic Composition School Type (type one - type two - type three - type four). This fourfold classification was based on the percentage of Mexican Americans in the total number of eighth grade respondents at a given school. Type four schools were those where Mexican Americans made up less than 25 percent of the entire number of respondents. Type three schools are those where Mexican Americans comprised between 25-49 percent. Type two schools are those where the total number of respondents was composed of between 50-74 percent Mexican American, and type one schools are those in which the Mexican Americans made up from 75-100 percent of the total respondents for the school.

Parentage of Respondent (MA-MA mother-MA father). Although all respondents included in the sample are Mexican Americans, for purposes of comparison on this variable individuals were separated into three categories. Respondents whose parents were both Mexican American were classified as MA, those whose mother was Mexican American but whose father was Anglo were classified as MA mother, and those whose father was Mexican American but whose mother was Anglo were classified as MA father.

The rationale for the selection of these eight variables is derived, for the most part, from the material presented in the sections dealing with related research and related theory. Each variable was chosen because of its possible or apparent influence on the assimilation process under consideration.

Sex was chosen because much previous research has shown females to be more conforming than males (Asch, 1956; Beloff, 1958; Tuddenham, 1958), and also more influenceable with regard to the modification of their beliefs and opinions (Janis and Field, 1959). This can be an important factor in the schools which have as an objective the Americanization of its pupils. In addition, Grebler, Moore, and Guzman report that women have a higher rate of exogamy than men (1970), and this is one specific aspect of assimilation being studied.

Religion has been recognized as an important element by Warner and Srole who use it as one of the factors to be considered in deciding the probability and speed of assimilation of a given immigrant group. In general, those of the same religion as the dominant group will be assimilated more easily and quickly (1945:295). Grebler, Moore, and Guzman note that among some of the Catholic hierarchy there is a feeling that Americanization contributes to the conversion of Mexican Americans to Protestantism (1970:461). They also write that Protestant missions have stated their dedication to Americanization through evangelization (1970:507). If certain denominations have assimilation or Americanization as an objective, then religion becomes an important considera-

30

tion.

Class is an important variable according to the previously presented theory of Alexander Weinstock who states that the higher the class of the individual the more acceptable he is and consequently the more rapid his assimilation (1964:321-40). As noted above, research also indicated that there tends to be an inverse relationship between class and traditional Mexican attitudes and behavior (Moore:127-33). A study by Mittlebach and Moore reveals that for Mexican Americans there is a direct relationship between class and exogamy (1968:54-61). These findings, therefore, indicate the possible existence of a relationship between class and various aspects of assimilation.

Religiosity was selected because of data presented in studies, as well as traditional sociological perspectives. Sociologists, working from the framework provided by Weber, have tended to see Catholicism as promoting a preoccupation with other worldly things. Assuming there is some validity in this perspective, it would be logical to further assume that the more one accepts Catholicism the more spiritual, otherworld directed, and non-materialistic that person would be. The orientation is generally away from that of the WASP which is recognized as more materialistic, and work-oriented. Therefore, it would be expected that the more religious a Catholic Mexican American is, the less he would be like the Protestant Anglo. Grebler, Moore, and Guzman, present the findings that Mexican Americans are less observant of religious beliefs and practices than Anglos (1970:449-77). The more religious a Mexican American is, therefore, the more he departs from the commonly found Mexican tradition, and the closer he moves to that of the Anglo. Any movement away from the "Mexican" toward the "Anglo" has implications for assimilation.

Aspirational level would seem to be rather closely related to education, occupation, and social mobility. Given the urbanized, industrialized nature of modern American society, high aspirations can only be fulfilled through education and a white collar or professional occupation which can lead to social mobility. As previously noted, the longer a Mexican American student is in a public school the more he is like the Anglo in values and expectations (Moore, 1970:83-84). Moore also reports that white collar Mexican Americans are most likely to mingle with Anglos, and that some upward mobile Mexicans marry Anglos for status or prestige. Data dealing with inter-marriage show that mobility may mean assimilation (1970:114). Grebler, Moore and Guzman state that findings of studies imply that the highest achievers are those Mexican Americans who have been most thoroughly socialized to the dominant Anglo culture (1970: 171).

School System Attendance Consistency, or the length of time a student spends in the public or parochial school system, had been shown to be important in other studies. For example, attitudes and beliefs vary according to the number of years spent in the parochial school system (Bressler and Westoff, 1963). The finding, mentioned above, that the farther a Mexican American student goes in a public school the more similar he becomes to the Anglo students also seems to indicate the importance of this variable (Moore, 1970:83-84).

Ethnic Composition School Type is relevant according to previously presented theories and research. Schermerhorn states in his theory that immigrant groups that concentrate together tend to perpetuate their native cultures, and that the greater a group disperses among the dominant group the more rapid will be its assimilation (1949: 460). This is also related to the theory of Robin Williams which contends that the larger the ratio of the immigrant group to the dominant group the slower will be its assimilation (1947:58). Research indicates that those Mexican Americans in San Antonio who live outside of the Mexican American ghetto in ethnically mixed neighborhoods have many more Anglo friends and also use them much more as a reference group than do Mexican Americans who live in the ghetto (Moore, 1970:111-12). Since San Antonio schools still operate on the neighborhood concept, the ethnic composition of the schools would reflect that of the neighborhood.

Parentage of Respondents is shown to be a relevant variable by the theory of Warner and Srole. They say that the lighter the skin color and more caucasoid appearing an individual is the more quickly and easily he will be assimilated (1945:295). Ordinarily, because of genetic mechanisms, children of Mexican-Anglo marriages would be more likely to exhibit these favored characteristics than would the children of all Mexican marriages. Research has also revealed that children having two Mexican American parents are more likely to speak Spanish than those having only one such parent (Moore, 1970:120). This, together with the finding that there is a direct relationship between amount of Spanish spoken and identification with participation in the Mexican American subculture (Nall, 1962:28-41; Penalosa and McDonagh, 1966:24), would indicate that children of endogamous marriages may be less assimilated than those of exogamous marriages.

- - - - -

Footnotes for this Chapter:

1. The major occupational categories are: treated as middle class (1) higher executives, proprietors of large concerns, and major professionals; (2) business managers, proprietors of medium-sized businesses and lesser professionals; (3) administrative personnel, proprietors of small independent businesses and minor professionals; (4) clerical and sales workers, technicians and owners of little businesses. Treated as working class (5) skilled manual employees; (6) machine operators and semiskilled employees; (7) unskilled employees.

CHAPTER IV

PRESENTATION AND ANALYSIS OF THE DATA

An Overview

Results of the study are presented and discussed in this chapter. Each of the hypotheses are considered in the order of their presentation in Chapter One. For ease of reading and understanding, each hypothesis is repeated in the text at the beginning of the exposition of data and discussion pertaining to it. The presentation includes the general findings by section as well as the results of introducing into the analysis each of the test variables. Interpretations and possible explanations of the data will be given in the discussions which immediately follow.

Asterisks have been used in the tables which accompany the discussion of each section. These are used to indicate those results which were found to be significant at the .05 level of confidence or better. Special attention will be called to those results which were significant at the .01 level or beyond.

The instrument was composed of seven sections each testing a different aspect of assimilation, and contained a total of sixty-six items. Results of Student's t test reveal that there was a significant difference between the responses of the Mexican Americans in public schools and those in parochial schools in six of the seven sections. Seven of the eight null hypotheses, therefore, were rejected.

It was found that not only was there a significant difference on six of the seven subtypes between degree of assimilation of Mexican American eighth grade students in parochial and their counterparts in public schools, but that in all but one case it was in favor of those in the church-related schools.

Similar results were achieved by the Mann-Whitney U test, which treats the data as ordinal level. Based on this test, six of the eight differences referred to above were found to be significant at the .05 level. Therefore, the conclusions reached regarding the acceptance or rejection of the null hypotheses were the same as those arrived at on the basis of the t test, with the exception of hypothesis five which was tested by Section 3. On this, the t test found the differences between the respondents from the two school systems to be significant at the .04 level of confidence while the U test found it to be significant at the .15 level. Refer to Table 7 for the complete results, including significance levels derived from both tests.

Table 6 on page 28 contains the correlation coefficient for each of the seven sections, and the grand total when compared to all other sections, and the grand total. The relative lack of significant correlations would indicate that the researcher was indeed measuring different aspects or subtypes of assimilation, as assumed.

TABLE 7

COMPARISON OF MEAN ASSIMILATION SCORES BY SECTION

| Section | School System | | | | Test | |
| | Public | | Parochial | | | |
	Mean	Var	Mean	Var	t	U
1	49.9	40.8	53.1	39.9	4.86***	4.56***
2	41.8	33.1	44.2	18.9	4.57***	4.72***
3	38.9	31.8	37.6	47.1	2.04*	1.45
4	27.2	25.4	27.4	29.1	0.27	0.61
5	31.5	22.6	33.7	17.8	4.84***	4.66***
6	16.3	11.4	17.0	10.8	2.03*	2.06*
7	7.1	12.4	8.1	9.2	2.79**	3.42***
Total Score	212.7	411.3	221.1	272.3	4.33**	4.61***

N=383
*Significant at .05 level
**Significant at .01 level
***Significant at .001 level

Hypothesis One

There is no difference in the degree of overall assimilation between eighth grade Mexican Americans in public schools and those in parochial schools.

This hypothesis was tested by means of the total scores for the entire questionnaire, thus comprising all seven sections with their seven separate aspects of assimilation.

Based on the results of Student's t test which yielded a value of 4.33 when comparing total mean scores for all Mexican Americans in public schools with those in parochial schools, this null hypothesis was not accepted (DF=383, p/.0001). Six of the seven sections showed a significant difference between the responses of the two groups. These six, in order of appearance in the questionnaire, are: acculturation, civic assimilation, identificational assimilation, attitude receptional assimilation, attitude toward amalgamation, and structural assimilation. The only section which failed to show a significant difference was that which dealt with behavior receptional assimilation. This means, therefore, that there is a difference in the degree of overall assimilation between eighth grade Mexican Americans in public schools and those in parochial schools.

Eighth grade Mexican American students in the parochial schools appear to be much more assimilated than their fellow ethnic group members in public schools. Not only did they have a higher total score, but they also scored higher on six of the seven sections, as can be seen in a comparison of the means. The only section on which the Mexican Americans in Public Schools scored higher was that dealing with identificational assimilation. For a more complete comparison refer to Table 7.

34

It is also of interest to note in the table that on five of the seven sections, the variance for Mexican Americans in public schools is larger than for those in parochial schools. This would indicate that there is, in general, a greater divergence of opinion among those in public schools in most areas under consideration. The exceptions were in Section III, which measured identificational assimilation, and Section IV, which measured behavior receptional assimilation.

When controlling for each of the test factors the results were generally the same although there was some variation. It should be noted that there is a general consistent pattern of higher assimilation scores for parochial school students in all subtypes except identificational assimilation which invariably favors public school respondents.

Controlling for Sex

Both males and females attending parochial schools had significantly higher means than their public school counterparts. The t value for males was 3.64, while for females it was 2.66. These values were significant at the .001 and .008 levels, respectively. Table 8 also shows that females in general, had higher means than males, and this difference was found to be significant at the .04 level.

TABLE 8

COMPARISON OF OVERALL ASSIMILATION BY SEX

	Means				
Sex	Public	Parochial	t	D.F.	Prob.
Males	209.0	219.9	3.64*	188	.001
Females	215.9	222.3	2.66*	195	.008
	Males	Females			
All Schools	215.4	219.4	2.07*	383	.04

*Significant

Controlling for Religion

Catholics in parochial schools showed a significantly greater degree of overall assimilation than those in public schools. The t value was 4.51 which is significant at the .0001 level. Although the difference was not significant, Catholics also had higher means than non-Catholics when they were compared regardless of school system. The data are presented in Table 9.

TABLE 9

COMPARISON OF OVERALL ASSIMILATION BY RELIGION

Religion	Means Public	Parochial	t	D.F.	Prob.
Catholic	212.6	221.1	4.51*	357	.0001
	Catholic	Non-Catholic			
All Schools	217.7	213.9	0.63	383	.53

*Significant

Due to the fact that there was only one non-Catholic in a parochial school, it was not possible to compare the responses of non-Catholics in the two school systems. As previously noted, there was relatively few non-Catholics (26) in the entire sample, but this is consistent with the national pattern for this ethnic group.

Controlling for Class

Table 10 reveals that whereas middle class students in public schools had somewhat higher means, among working class students it was those from parochial schools who enjoyed higher mean scores. However, only the difference between working class respondents was significant with a t value of 4.23. This was significant at the .0001 level.

TABLE 10

COMPARISON OF OVERALL ASSIMILATION BY CLASS

Class	Means Public	Parochial	t	D.F.	Prob.
Middle	222.3	221.7	0.14	119	.88
Working	211.1	221.1	4.23*	224	.0001
	Middle	Working			
All Schools	221.8	215.9	2.92*	363	.004

*Significant

When respondents from the two SES groups were compared regardless of their school system, the middle class showed a significantly greater degree of assimilation. The resulting t value was 2.92 which is significant at the .004 level.

36

Controlling for Religiosity

Students were classified high, medium or low depending on their responses to the questions regarding the frequency of church attendance, family prayer, Bible reading, and whether or not they received religious instruction and religious training. Parochial school respondents classified high and medium had higher means, but only for the latter group was the difference significant. The t of 3.43 was significant at the .001 level. It was not possible to compare those from the two school systems who were classified as low in RE due to the fact that only one individual was so classified in parochial schools. As can be seen in Table 11, when comparing groups regardless of school attended, a direct relationship appeared between RE and assimilation.

TABLE 11

COMPARISON OF OVERALL ASSIMILATION BY RELIGIOSITY

Religiosity	Means		t	D.F. ·	Prob.
	Public	Parochial			
High	221.0	221.8	0.22	121	.82
Medium	211.9	220.7	3.43*	221	.001
	High	Medium			
All Schools	221.5	217.4	1.94*	342	.05
	Medium	Low			
All Schools	217.4	205.7	4.21*	262	.0001

*Significant

It should be noted that the distribution of parochial school respondents in terms of RE is skewed to the high side, while that of the public school respondents is normal. Of the 215 parochial respondents 36 percent were classified high and 64 percent medium. The 168 public respondents were classified as follows: 26 percent high, 50 percent medium, 24 percent low.

Controlling for Aspirational Level

Three categories, high, medium and low, were utilized, with the criteria for classifying individuals being their responses to the questions regarding desire to attend college, probability of attending, and desired future career. Respondents in all three classifications from parochial schools showed a greater degree of assimilation, and differences between the school systems were significant in two of the comparisons. Comparing the high groups resulted in a t value of 2.09, significant at the .04 level, while comparing those medium revealed a t of 3.01, significant at the .004 level. An inter-group comparison revealed a direct relationship between AL and assimilation. The difference between the high and medium groups was significant at the .0001 level, as was that between the medium and low groups. The data are presented in Table 12.

Controlling for School System Attendance Consistency

Respondents were placed into one of three categories depending on the length of time they had been in the school system currently attended. Those who had spent at least two-thirds of their time in the same system were classified as high, between two-thirds and one-third were medium, and less than one-third were low. It is shown in

TABLE 12

COMPARISON OF OVERALL ASSIMILATION BY ASPIRATIONAL LEVEL

Aspirational Level	Means Public	Parochial	t	D.F.	Prob.
High	218.2	223.2	2.09*	231	.04
Medium	208.8	218.4	3.01*	132	.004
Low	196.6	204.0	1.17	20	.26
	High	Medium			
All Schools	221.3	213.3	3.95*	363	.0001
	Medium	Low			
All Schools	213.3	199.6	4.03*	152	.0001

*Significant

Table 13 that high and medium SSAC respondents from parochial schools had higher mean scores, with the difference between the former groups being very significant. A t value of 4.75 resulted which was significant beyond the .0001 level. There were too few respondents (3) classified as low in public schools to allow a comparison to be made. Most students from both systems had spent virtually their entire school career in the same system.

In addition to the above, a comparison was also made within each school system. Results of comparisons in the parochial school system indicated a direct relationship between SSAC and assimilation while in the public school system there was no difference between those classified high and medium.

TABLE 13

COMPARISON OF OVERALL ASSIMILATION BY SCHOOL
SYSTEM ATTENDANCE CONSISTENCY

SSAC	Means Public	Parochial	t	D.F.	Prob.
High	212.5	222.2	4.75*	331	.0001
Medium	212.6	220.4	1.06	29	.30
	High	Medium			
Public	212.5	212.6	0.01	165	.99
Parochial	222.2	220.4	0.54	195	.60
	Medium	Low			
Parochial	220.4	212.0	1.62	38	.11

*Significant

Controlling for Ethnic Composition School Type

The schools themselves were classified as types 1, 2, 3 or 4 ECST depending on the percentage of Mexican Americans represented among the respondents. Type 1 schools were those which had the highest percentage while type 4 schools were those with the lowest. Table 14 shows that parochial school respondents from type 1 ECST schools had higher means. The difference between the means of the two groups attending schools at least 75 percent Mexican American was extremely significant, the t of 7.71 was well beyond the .0001 level. There were no types 3 or 4 parochial schools, since all were at least 50 percent Mexican American, and only one of each type was found among the public schools.

In both school systems there was a direct relationship between percentage of Anglos in the class and the assimilation of the Mexican American respondents. Differences between respondents from the various type schools were very significant within the public system, but not within the parochial system.

TABLE 14

COMPARISON OF OVERALL ASSIMILATION BY
ETHNIC COMPOSITION SCHOOL TYPE

ECST	Means Public	Parochial	t	D.F.	Prob.
Type 1	204.0	220.8	7.71*	256	.0001
Type 2	223.3	221.8	0.48	116	.65
	Type 1	Type 2			
Public	204.0	223.3	6.58*	157	.0001
Parochial	220.8	221.8	0.42	215	.68
	Type 2	Type 3			
Public	223.3	234.7	2.57*	68	.01

*Significant

Controlling for Parentage of Respondents

All respondents fell into one of three groups, depending on the ethnic background of their parents. It was of interest to see what, if any, was the difference between children of endogamous and exogamous marriages. More specifically, the question was whether there was a noticeable difference in responses between those whose parents were both Mexican American, those who had an Anglo father and a Mexican American mother, and those who had a Mexican American father, and an Anglo mother. All but thirty-one of the respondents had parents who were both Mexican American. The fewest number (8) had a Mexican American father and an Anglo mother.

TABLE 15

COMPARISON OF OVERALL ASSIMILATION BY PARENTAGE OF RESPONDENTS

Parentage of Respondents	Means Public	Parochial	t	D.F.	Prob.
Both MA	210.3	221.1	5.62*	352	.0001
MA Mother	239.9	222.2	3.12*	23	.005
MA Father	254.4	214.8	4.00*	8	.00=

*Significant

A comparison between those students whose parents were both Mexican American indicated a significant advantage for parochial school respondents. A t value of 5.62 was obtained, which was significant at the .0001 level. However, Table 15 reveals that when either parent was Anglo, public school respondents had higher mean scores. This

40

was a reversal of the previously consistent pattern which favored Mexican Americans from parochial schools. The difference between those with MA mothers was significant at .005 level and for MA fathers it was at the .007 level.

Discussion

In all of the above comparisons two rather consistent patterns emerged. First, parochial school students showed a greater degree of assimilation. Second, public school respondents scored higher on identificational assimilation and were more or less even on behavior receptional assimilation.

It is immediately evident from the data presented that there is indeed a difference in the degree of overall assimilation between eighth grade Mexican Americans in public schools, and those in parochial schools. Not only are the differences in responses on thirteen of the eighteen total mean scores presented above significantly different, but also of importance is the general consistent pattern which emerges favoring those in parochial schools.

From the foregoing, it appears that parochial school Mexican Americans are, on the average, more assimilated than those in public schools, and this relationship between school system and assimilation persists even when other variables are controlled. It would seem that there are several reasons for this. In general, private schools enjoy a higher status, and are thus able to confer greater prestige on their students and graduates, than public schools. Since not everyone can or will enter a private school there is a type of self selection at work, which results in an uneven distribution of "high strivers" in such schools. The schools themselves are committed to the ideal of offering the students a better and more personalized education than is possible to achieve in public schools. This ideal is generally reflected in the recruitment and employment of the school's faculty, who in turn, reflect it in the classroom. In the concrete situation, this commitment to the betterment of the students may lead, consciously or unconsciously, to the "Anglicization" or "Americanization" of them since this is what will be rewarded in and by society.

In addition, in the case of parochial schools, there may be other factors working which tend to maximize this assimilative effect. All students, regardless of minority group membership, are accepted and united through Catholicism. Given this common bond and identity, together with the small size of the school, which does not allow students to group together in ethnic enclaves, the result is greater structural assimilation, which as Gordon has pointed out leads to all other types of assimilation (1964:81).

As noted above, the finding that females appeared to be more assimilated than males is consistent with previous research. In a brief survey of related research Marlowe and Gergen (1969:617) noted that in the 1950's Applezweig and Moeller, Beloff, Asch, Crutchfield, and Tuddenham all reported that women are more conforming than men, and Janis and Field found them more influenceable with regard to the modification of their beliefs and opinions. They attribute this, at least in part, to the differential socialization of males and females, particularly to the different characteristics which are valued in each.

Closely related to this as a possible factor is the concept of machismo, which has been identified by most writers as an important element in the Mexican culture. Aspects of machismo such as individualism, courage, leadership, loyalty to your group, etc., may act as obstacles for the males which impede their assimilation. Becoming "anglicized" might be seen as, at best, a compromise, or at worst, a betrayal of their Mexican heritage. Those who are too "Anglo" are frequently chided for being a "tio taco" (Mexican Uncle Tom) or a "coconut" (brown on the outside but white on the inside).

Since machismo is not expected of, nor prized by, the females, it could be expected that they would be more assimilated.

The greater assimilation of the Catholics over the non-Catholics may be explained, in part, by the fact that in San Antonio Protestant churches, which do not service specific territorially defined parishes as do Catholic churches, tend to be more racially and ethnically segregated. Churches which service Protestant Mexican Americans are usually headed by a Mexican American minister who speaks to them in Spanish. Their common Mexican heritage is used as a recruiting device, making membership in their particular church more attractive. In general, Protestant Mexican Americans tend to be rather isolated, both from the majority of Mexican Americans who are Catholics, and from the majority of Protestants who are Anglos. This isolation causes them to rely on their fellow church members to satisfy all their social and emotional needs. The overall result is a strengthening or reinforcement of their subcultural differences. This agrees with findings of Margaret Sumner (1970:225-33).

Given the fact that our core society is basically middle class it is not surprising that middle class Mexican Americans were more assimilated than those in the working class. Particularly since "Each class is a subculture, with a set of attitudes, beliefs, values, and behavior norms which differ from those of other classes" (Horton and Hung, 1972:273).

A possible factor in explaining the finding that there was a direct relation between religiosity and assimilation, so that the higher the respondents scored on religiosity the more assimilated they tended to be, can be found in the writings of Will Herberg (1955). He points out that religion in the United States has become Americanized. This goes beyond the mere idea that a religion is embodied in a concrete (cultural) way. Herberg means that many American values, ideas, etc., which are not per se religious in nature, such as the superiority of democracy, religious pluralism, separation of Church and State, etc., have in effect been sanctified and incorporated into our religious beliefs. Assuming the correctness of this assertion it would follow that as a person became more religious he would at the same time become more Americanized. Since this crosscuts all denominations and sects the result is that in the United States an individual who is highly religious is also highly American. People, regardless of their specific religious affiliation, therefore, are brought together into the "American way" which is basically the Anglo way.

As with religiosity, the data indicated there was a direct relation between aspirational level and degree of assimilation. This was to be expected since desire to get ahead in an Anglo society requires some knowledge of, and conformity to, the dominant group which controls the rewards and opportunities sought. The respondents, being so young, may well have been reflecting the aspirations and responding to the encouragement of their parents, who if they realistically wanted to give their children a chance of realizing their goals would be forced to prepare them properly. This preparation would include learning to think and act in a socially accepted and rewarded way, i.e., the Anglo way.

Assuming the difference in degree of assimilation between students of the two school systems which may have been the result of attending the schools prompted the inclusion of school system attendance consistency as a test variable. It was reasoned that if one school system was superior to the other in promoting the assimilation of its minority group pupils, then degree of assimilation should be directly related to years of attendance in the "superior" system. This means, concretely, that the respective order for the most assimilated students in relation to SSAC should be high, medium, low in the "superior" assimilation-promoting school system, but in the "inferior" assimilation-promoting system it should be low, medium, and high.

This, indeed, appears to be what the data indicated, although in most cases rather weakly. Nevertheless, the direction is consistent. In public schools the group classified as medium in SSAC had a higher total mean score, although just barely, than those classified as high.

When comparing those parochial school respondents high in SSAC with those low the trend was very clear and definite. Respondents classified high had a total mean assimilation score that was significantly higher than the respondents classified low. The former group also had higher mean scores on all of the subtypes of assimilation, although in only three cases were the differences significant.

In summary, therefore, it was found that in public schools, whose students consistently scored lower in assimilation throughout the analysis, there obtained an inverse relationship, although very weak, between SSAC and assimilation. On the other hand, in parochial schools, whose students were consistently higher in assimilation, there was a direct relationship between SSAC and assimilation. Thus, based on total mean assimilation scores it was found that the respective order for the more assimilated respondents in relation to SSAC was medium, high, in public schools, while in the parochial schools it was high, medium, low. This finding appears to strengthen the conclusion that there is a difference in degree of assimilation between public and parochial school students, and that there is something in the parochial schools which promotes greater assimilation of its Mexican American pupils.

Next, the finding that there is an inverse relationship between ECST and assimilation, such that the smaller the percentage of Mexican Americans in the class, the greater is their assimilation was to be expected. These results are consistent with the above cited theory of Schermerhorn, and the previously presented data that Mexican Americans in San Antonio who live in the frontier, as opposed to the colony, are more likely to use Anglos as both a membership group and as a reference group.

All of the data discussed to this point reveal that while there are differences in degree of assimilation according to the stratified test variable, the overall differences in all cases favor those in parochial schools. There was an attempt made to explain this difference at the beginning of the present discussion. Now, however, one is faced with a complete reversal of the previous pattern of responses. When controlling for the parentage of respondents it was found that children of ethnically exogamous marriages in public schools are more assimilated than their counterparts in parochial schools. While it should be noted that the differences, in most cases, were not found to be significant, the change of higher means in favor of the public schools is striking.

This apparent change may be spurious and due to the small sample size, but, assuming it is real an attempt should be made to explain it. The answer may lie in the statement by Simpson and Yinger that "Public-school systems are responsive to the dominant social influences of the communities of which they are parts; their operations cannot be understood unless this point is grasped" (1958:611). Although the authors were not talking about assimilation of minority group students, it is felt that the point they make is applicable. Public schools, represented by administrators and teachers, are extremely aware of and guided by the general feelings of the communities of which they are parts. When making the necessary arrangements to collect the data this researcher found a very noticeable difference between the apparent concern for community and parental opinion displayed by the administrators of public and parochial schools. The former openly expressed much more concern for the opinions and reactions of the community.

It is easy to understand this situation when one remembers that the continued employment of public school personnel depends more directly on the acceptance and good will of the public than does that of parochial school personnel. Thus, if an Anglo is more acceptable than a Mexican American, and a half-Anglo half-Mexican American is more acceptable than a full Mexican American in the community, we would expect this to be reflected in the public schools more than in the parochial schools.

Hypothesis Two

> There is no difference in the degree of acculturation between Mexican Americans in the eighth grade in public schools and those in parochial schools.

This hypothesis was tested by means of sixteen different items, each of which revealed something in the respondents' attitudes, values or feelings regarding certain aspects of our American culture.

Based on the results of Student's t this null hypothesis was rejected, with a t value of 4.86 (D.F.=383, p/.0001). This, of course, means that there is a significant difference between the degree of cultural assimilation of the eighth grade Mexican American students in public schools and those in parochial schools. Contrary to what might have been expected based on what little could be found on this subject, there is a difference and that difference in acculturation favors those students in parochial schools.

TABLE 16

SECTION I COMPARISON OF RESULTS BY ITEM

| Item | Public | | Parochial | | |
	Mean	S.D.	Mean	S.D.	t
1	1.74	0.90	1.85	1.00	1.2
2	3.29	1.22	3.75	1.24	3.7**
3	3.41	1.16	3.42	1.15	0.1
4	4.23	0.89	4.07	1.03	1.6
5	2.98	1.20	3.35	1.11	3.1**
6	3.06	1.33	3.44	1.30	2.8**
7	2.27	1.07	2.61	1.24	2.8**
8	4.30	0.90	4.46	0.76	1.8
9	2.97	1.42	3.09	1.23	0.9
10	3.03	1.22	3.30	1.05	2.3*
11	4.07	1.00	4.04	1.03	0.3
12	3.13	1.24	3.44	1.24	2.4**
13	2.36	1.20	2.49	1.32	1.0
14	2.58	1.04	2.96	1.05	3.6**
15	2.95	1.24	3.01	1.09	0.5
16	3.51	1.30	3.78	1.27	2.0*

N=383
*Significant at .05 level
**Significant at .01 level

44

As can be seen in Table 16, of the sixteen items which comprised Section I, upon which hypothesis two is based, parochial school Mexican American students had higher mean assimilation scores on fourteen of them. Differences between means proved to be significant on eight of the sixteen items.

Controlling for Sex

Males from parochial schools appeared to be significantly more acculturated than those from public schools. Comparing the difference between their means resulted in a t of 4.33 which was significant at the .0001 level. Although the difference was not as great, parochial school females were also significantly more assimilated. The t of 2.56 was significant at the .01 level. In addition, Table 17 reveals that when all males and females were compared, regardless of school system, females had higher mean scores. The difference, however, was not significant.

TABLE 17

COMPARISON OF ACCULTURATION BY SEX

Sex	Means Public	Parochial	t	D.F.	Prob.
Males	48.6	53.1	4.33*	188	.0001
Females	51.0	53.0	2.56*	195	.01
	Males	Females			
All Schools	51.2	52.1	1.30	383	.19

*Significant

Controlling for Religion

Catholic respondents from parochial schools had significantly higher means than their public school counterparts. A t value of 4.38 resulted from the comparison, which was significant at the .0001 level. When all Catholics were compared with all non-Catholics, without controlling for school system, it was found that Catholics enjoyed higher means. Complete results can be seen in Table 18.

TABLE 18

COMPARISON OF ACCULTURATION BY RELIGION

Religion	Means		t	D.F.	Prob.
	Public	Parochial			
Catholic	50.2	53.0	4.38*	357	.0001
	Catholic	Non-Catholic			
All Schools	51.9	48.7	1.70	383	.09

*Significant

Controlling for Class

Both middle and working class respondents attending parochial schools showed higher means than the corresponding groups from public schools. Only the difference between working class groups was significant, with a t value of 3.96. This was found to be significant at the .0001 level. As can be seen in Table 19, the middle class

TABLE 19

COMPARISON OF ACCULTURATION BY CLASS

Class	Means		t	D.F.	Prob.
	Public	Parochial			
Middle	51.4	52.9	1.17	119	.24
Working	50.1	53.3	3.96*	244	.0001
	Middle	Working			
All Schools	52.6	51.6	1.30	363	.19

*Significant

respondents had higher means than those in the working class when these two groups were compared without regard for school system.

Controlling for Religiosity

Parochial school students classified as high and medium in RE had higher means than those similarly classified in public schools. The difference between the medium groups was significant at the .0001 level with a t value of 4.06. Table 20 also shows that when comparing those high with those medium, regardless of school

TABLE 20

COMPARISON OF ACCULTURATION BY RELIGIOSITY

Religiosity	Means Public	Parochial	t	D.F.	Prob.
High	51.3	52.9	1.43	121	.15
Medium	49.3	53.2	4.06*	221	.0001
	High	Medium			
All Schools	52.3	51.7	0.78	342	.44
	Medium	Low			
All Schools	51.7	49.6	2.29*	262	.02

*Significant

system, the high group enjoyed an advantage. The medium group, however, was signifi- cantly more acculturated than the low group. The t value was 2.29 which was signifi- cant at the .02 level.

Controlling for Aspirational Level

Table 21 reveals that both high and medium respondents from parochial schools were significantly more acculturated than their public school counterparts. A t value of 2.97, significant at the .004 level, resulted from a comparison of the high groups, while a t of 2.87, significant at the .005 level, was obtained when comparing the med- ium groups. Although the difference was not significant, parochial school respondents low in AL also had higher means.

Comparing means for all high AL individuals with those of all medium, and all medium with all low yielded significant differences indicating the existence of a direct relationship between aspiration and acculturation. For the former comparison the t value of 3.72 was significant at the .0001 level, and for the latter the t of 3.26 was significant at the .002 level. This same direct relationship is also found within both school systems.

TABLE 21

COMPARISON OF ACCULTURATION BY ASPIRATIONAL LEVEL

Aspirational Level	Means Public	Parochial	t	D.F.	Prob.
High	51.4	53.8	2.97*	231	.004
Medium	49.0	52.0	2.87*	132	.005
Low	44.2	47.6	1.21	20	.24
	High	Medium			
All Schools	52.9	50.4	3.72*	363	.0001
	Medium	Low			
All Schools	50.4	45.5	3.26*	152	.002

*Significant

TABLE 22

COMPARISON OF ACCULTURATION BY SCHOOL SYSTEM ATTENDANCE CONSISTENCY

SSAC	Means Public	Parochial	t	D.F.	Prob.
High	49.7	53.3	5.22*	331	.0001
Medium	52.2	51.9	0.08	29	.94
	High	Medium			
Public	49.7	52.2	0.97	165	.34
Parochial	53.3	51.9	0.78	195	.44
	Medium	Low			
Parochial	51.9	52.1	0.07	38	.94

*Significant

Controlling for School System Attendance Consistency

Parochial school respondents had higher means only in the first of the two inter-system comparisons. The t value of 5.22, significant beyond the .0001 level, was obtained when comparing the high groups, but this was in sharp contrast to the virtual lack of difference between the medium groups. Refer to Table 22 for the complete results.

Making intra-system comparisons revealed a difference in the two systems. The medium group had a higher means than the high group in the public schools, while the reverse was true in the parochial schools. In parochial schools the medium group showed a slightly lower means than the low group. Based on the only comparison possible in public there appears to be an inverse relationship between length of attendance and acculturation, whereas in parochial schools the results are not as clear.

Controlling for Ethnic Composition School Type

Inter-system comparisons between the two type 1 groups, as well as the two type 2 groups indicated that parochial school respondents were more acculturated. The former comparison yielded a t of 5.18, which was significant beyond the .0001 level. From Table 23 it can be seen that there was also a significant difference between the

TABLE 23

COMPARISON OF ACCULTURATION BY ETHNIC COMPOSITION SCHOOL TYPE

ECST	Means Public	Parochial	t	D.F.	Prob.
Type 1	48.7	53.0	5.18*	256	.0001
Type 2	51.7	53.3	1.30	116	.19
	Type 1	Type 2			
Public	48.7	51.7	2.98*	157	.004
Parochial	53.0	53.3	0.27	215	.78
	Type 2	Type 3			
Public	51.7	51.3	0.23	68	.82

*Significant

type 1 and type 2 public school groups. The t value of 2.98, which favored the group classified type 2, was found to be significant at the .004 level. This same group also had higher means than type 3 group. In parochial schools the type 2 group had a slightly higher means than the type 1 group. Therefore, in both school systems respondents in the schools with the highest percentage of Mexican American pupils were the least acculturated.

Controlling for Parentage of Respondents

Table 24 reveals that respondents from parochial schools whose parents are both Mexican Americans enjoyed significantly higher means than their public school counterparts. The t of 5.27 was significant beyond the .0001 level. However, the comparisons involving children of ethnically mixed marriages favored the public school students.

TABLE 24

COMPARISON OF ACCULTURATION BY PARENTAGE OF RESPONDENTS

Parentage of Respondents	Means		t	D.F.	Prob.
	Public	Parochial			
Both MA	49.6	53.2	5.27*	352	.0001
MA Mother	52.9	51.9	0.41	23	.69
MA Father	53.8	50.8	0.68	8	.53

*Significant

Discussion

A consistent pattern of greater acculturation on the part of parochial school students was very apparent, and could be seen in the fact that the overall difference was significant at the .0001 level. Possible reasons for this were presented in the previous discussion.

Differences between males and females were not nearly as great on acculturation as for total assimilation. Intra-sex comparisons between parochial and public schools favored the former in both cases. The same thing occurred in intra-religious comparisons, involving Catholics. Catholics, in general, were found to be more acculturated than non-Catholics.

It made no real difference in the outcome whether SES, RE, AL, SSAC or ECST were controlled. In all cases parochial school respondents showed greater acculturation. Note should be taken of the fact that those who spent from two-thirds to one hundred percent of their entire grade school career in a public school were less acculturated than their fellow classmates who had transferred in from a parochial school after having spent at least one-third of their career in such a school. The opposite is true of those in parochial schools. Students who had spent from two-thirds to all of their careers in a parochial school were more acculturated than their classmates who transferred in from public schools, and the longer they had spent in such schools the relatively less acculturated they were.

As we noted in the previous discussion of hypothesis one, the pattern changes when dealing with Mexican Americans from ethnically mixed marriages. Respondents with an Anglo father and Mexican American mother, thus having an Anglo surname, were more acculturated in public schools than in parochial schools. In the reverse type of ethnically mixed marriage the public school respondents were again slightly favored in total acculturation mean score. Besides the advantage that these students enjoyed over their parochial school counterparts, they enjoy an even greater one over their fellow students whose parents are both Mexican American.

Hypothesis Three

There is no difference in the degree of structural assimilation between eighth grade Mexican Americans in public schools and those in parochial schools.

This hypothesis was tested by means of four separate items, each of which measured the degree to which the respondent was actually involved in social relationships with members of the dominant ethnic group. The data were elicited in Section VII of the questionnaire.

Based on the results of Student's t, this null hypothesis was also rejected. The t value was 2.79 (D.F.=383, p/.006). This means, therefore, that there is a significant difference in the degree of structural assimilation between those eighth grade Mexican Americans in parochial schools and those in public schools. Again, it is the Mexican Americans in the parochial schools who appear to be more assimilated.

Table 25 shows the complete results of Section VII and reveals that of the four items in this section, the parochial school Mexican Americans had higher mean

TABLE 25

SECTION VII COMPARISON OF RESULTS BY ITEM

| Item | Public | | Parochial | | |
	Mean	S.D.	Mean	S.D.	t
1	1.50	0.92	1.52	0.85	0.2
2	1.46	0.92	1.65	1.06	1.9
3	1.49	0.94	1.52	0.85	0.3
4	2.67	1.94	3.39	1.89	3.6**

N=383
*Significant at .05 level
**Significant at .01 level

scores on all of them. This indicated that these respondents are more structurally assimilated. When comparing the differences in responses between both Mexican American groups, one of the items was found to be significant at the .001 level, and another reached .06.

Controlling for Sex

Males and females from parochial schools showed greater structural assimilation than those from public schools. The difference between males was significant at the .03 level based on a t value of 2.21. Refer to Table 26 for complete results.

TABLE 26

COMPARISON OF STRUCTURAL ASSIMILATION BY SEX

Sex	Means		t	D.F.	Prob.
	Public	Parochial			
Male	6.9	7.9	2.21*	189	.03
Female	7.3	8.2	1.84	195	.06
	Male	Female			
All Schools	7.5	7.8	0.95	383	.34

*Significant

When comparing all males and females, regardless of school system, it was found that females had a higher mean score.

Controlling for Religion

There was a significant difference between the means of public and parochial school Catholics, with the latter enjoying the advantage. The t value of 2.96 was significant at the .004 level. There was virtually no difference, however, between Catholics and non-Catholics when those from the two systems were combined and compared. See Table 27 below.

TABLE 27

COMPARISON OF STRUCTURAL ASSIMILATION BY RELIGION

Religion	Means		t	D.F.	Prob.
	Public	Parochial			
Catholic	7.0	8.1	2.96*	357	.004
	Catholic	Non-Catholic			
All Schools	7.7	7.7	0.02	383	.98

*Significant

Controlling for Class

It can be seen in Table 28 that although the differences were not significant, both middle and working class respondents from parochial schools had higher mean scores than those from public schools.

TABLE 28

COMPARISON OF ASSIMILATION BY CLASS

Class	Means		t	D.F.	Prob.
	Public	Parochial			
Middle	8.0	8.8	0.90	119	.28
Working	7.1	7.6	1.27	244	.20
	Middle	Working			
All Schools	8.6	7.3	3.40*	363	.001

*Significant

A comparison of all middle and working class students, without regard for school system, revealed that middle class respondents exhibited a significantly greater degree of structural assimilation. The t value of 3.40 was found to be significant at the .001 level. Differences on three of the four items which comprised the section were significant at or beyond the .01 level. It will be noted that there is a direct relationship between SES and structural assimilation, both overall and within each school system.

Controlling for Religiosity

Public school respondents classified as high had a somewhat higher means than their parochial school counterparts. However, the medium group from parochial schools showed a significantly higher means than those similarly classified in public schools. The difference between the groups resulted in a t of 2.42 which was significant at the .02 level. Table 29 reveals that there is a direct relationship between religiosity and structural assimilation. When comparing all high with medium RE respondents, regardless of school system, and medium with low, it was found that in each case the higher of the two groups had higher means. The latter comparison yielded a t value of 2.65 which was significant at the .008 level.

53

TABLE 29

COMPARISON OF STRUCTURAL ASSIMILATION BY RELIGIOSITY

Religiosity	Means		t	D.F.	Prob.
	Public	Parochial			
High	8.4	8.1	0.52	121	.61
Medium	6.9	8.0	2.42*	221	.02
	High	Medium			
All Schools	8.2	7.6	1.65	342	.10
	Medium	Low			
All Schools	7.6	6.3	2.65*	262	.008

*Significant

Controlling for Aspirational Level

Parochial school respondents in all three categories, high, medium, and low, had higher mean scores than those in public schools. Only the difference between the

TABLE 30

COMPARISON OF STRUCTURAL ASSIMILATION BY ASPIRATIONAL LEVEL

Aspirational Level	Means		t	D.F.	Prob.
	Public	Parochial			
High	7.6	8.2	1.49	231	.14
Medium	7.1	8.0	1.46	132	.14
Low	4.2	6.3	2.11*	20	.05
	High	Medium			
All Schools	8.0	7.5	1.31	363	.19
	Medium	Low			
All Schools	7.5	5.1	4.44*	152	.0001

*Significant

54

low groups was significant, with a t of 2.11. This was significant at the .05 level, as can be seen in Table 30. It can also be seen in the table that there is a direct relationship between aspiration and structural assimilation for the sample as a whole as well as within each school system. When everyone from both school systems was combined and then compared on the basis of the three categories to which they were assigned, the direct relationship was apparent. The medium group showed a significantly greater degree of structural assimilation than did the low group. Not only was the t value of 4.44 significant beyond the .0001 level, but three of the four items exhibited significant differences at or beyond the .01 level.

Controlling for School System Attendance Consistency

Table 31 shows that all but one of the comparisons controlling for SSAC revealed differences which were significant. Both high and medium parochial school students enjoyed higher means than their public school counterparts. The resulting values of t were 2.95, significant at the .004 level, and 2.81, significant at the .009 level, respectively.

Intra-system comparisons within the public school system revealed that the high group had a significantly higher means than the medium group. The t of 2.13 was significant at the .03 level. In the parochial school system the medium group had a slight advantage over the high group, but a significant one, at the .05 level, over the low group.

Controlling for Ethnic Composition School Type

Most comparisons controlling for this variable resulted in a very significant difference. Respondents from types 1 and 2 parochial schools showed a significantly

TABLE 31

COMPARISON OF STRUCTURAL ASSIMILATION BY
SCHOOL SYSTEM ATTENDANCE CONSISTENCY

SSAC	Means Public	Parochial	t	D.F.	Prob.
High	7.2	8.2	2.95*	331	.004
Medium	5.6	8.3	2.81*	29	.009
	High	Medium			
Public	7.2	5.6	2.13*	165	.03
Parochial	8.2	8.3	0.10	195	.92
	Medium	High			
Parochial	8.3	6.5	1.97*	38	.05

*Significant

55

greater degree of structural assimilation than did those from public schools. For type 1 schools the t was 6.77 which was significant beyond the .0001 level, while for type 2 schools the t of 1.41 was not found to be significant. In addition to the extremely large difference between means in the former comparison it was also found that the differences on every item of the section were significant at the .001 level or beyond. In Table 32 it can be seen that the intra-system comparisons between respondents from types 1 and 2, and 2 and 3 schools revealed that an inverse relationship existed in both public and parochial schools between ECST and structural assimilation. In the public schools the differences between type 1 and 2 school respondents were significant on all four items of the section at or beyond the .0001 level.

TABLE 32

COMPARISON OF STRUCTURAL ASSIMILATION BY
ETHNIC COMPOSITION SCHOOL TYPE

| | Means | | | | |
ECST	Public	Parochial	t	D.F.	Prob.
Type 1	5.5	7.6	6.77*	256	.0001
Type 2	8.7	9.5	1.41	116	.16
	Type 1	Type 2			
Public	5.5	8.7	7.07*	157	.0001
Parochial	7.6	9.5	4.10*	215	.0001
	Type 2	Type 3			
Public	8.7	13.7	3.26*	68	.002

*Significant

Controlling for Parentage of Respondents

There was a very significant difference between the means of the parochial school respondents with Mexican American parents and the corresponding individuals in public schools. The resulting t value of 3.82, significant at the .0001 level, favored those in parochial schools. However, as Table 33 indicates, respondents from public schools who had an Anglo parent exhibited higher means than those from parochial schools. It will be noted that the greatest degree of structural assimilation was shown by public school Mexican Americans who had an Anglo mother, while their parochial school counterparts showed the least degree. The difference between the two groups, however, was not significant and may be due, at least in part, to the small number of students in these groups.

TABLE 33

COMPARISON OF STRUCTURAL ASSIMILATION
BY PARENTAGE OF RESPONDENTS

Parentage of Respondents	Means Public	Parochial	t	D.F.	Prob.
Both MA	6.7	8.0	3.82*	352	.0001
MA Mother	11.7	9.8	1.28	23	.21
MA Father	12.1	5.8	2.13	8	.08

*Significant

Discussion

The same pattern previously noted emerged again in this section, namely respondents from parochial school exhibit greater assimilation. Introduction of the various control factors into the analysis did not, in general, change this phenomenon. There were, nevertheless, several exceptions which should be noted.

When controlling for RE it was found that those in public schools classified as high showed slightly greater structural assimilation than their counterparts in parochial schools. The same was not true, however, for those classified as medium. For this category it was those in parochial schools who showed greater assimilation, and the difference was significant. Therefore, it would appear that this slight advantage, which was not significant, in favor of public school students high in RE was not a function of religiosity, or at least not religiosity alone, since it did not hold for those medium in RE as might be expected.

A possible explanation might be found in the type of religiosity involved. First, it should be remembered that the comparison did not deal with a Catholic-Protestant dichotomy, since virtually all of the respondents were Catholics. Therefore it is probably not a denominational difference, and since in this case, only the high RE category was dealt with, it was not a matter of degree of religiosity. What may have been involved was a difference in orientation or type or religiosity; i.e., traditional old Catholic or modern-ecumenical Catholic. It may be expected that a respondent from a modern-ecumenical-Catholic family background would be more open to structural assimilation than one from a more traditional old Catholic family, which at the same time would possibly tend to be more traditionally Mexican. It is this latter family which would be more likely to make the financial sacrifice to send their children to a parochial school.

In this section the effect of ECST was very striking. There was a very significant inverse relationship found to obtain between the proportion of Mexican Americans in a class and the degree of structural assimilation exhibited by the minority group student. It appears that the fewer fellow-ethnic group members there are available, the more the individual Mexican American student turns to the Anglo for primary relationships.

Once again it was found that children from ethnically exogamous marriages are more assimilated in public schools than in parochial schools. It does not matter which parent is Anglo, the mere fact that one is appears to be sufficient to promote structural assimilation.

Hypothesis Four

There is no difference in the attitude toward amalgamation between Mexican Americans in the eighth grade in public schools and those in parochial schools.

The hypothesis was tested in Section VI by means of seven items. These items were designed to indicate the degree to which the respondent tends towards, or is in favor of, amalgamation. In addition to containing statements which examined attitudes toward inter-ethnic dating and marriage, there were also items which elicited actual dating practices.

TABLE 34

SECTION VI COMPARISON OF RESULTS BY ITEM

| Item | Public | | Parochial | | |
	Mean	S.D.	Mean	S.D.	t
1	1.24	0.83	1.28	0.81	0.6
2	1.17	0.66	1.50	1.15	3.5**
3	1.36	0.99	1.51	0.99	1.5
4	3.55	1.13	4.00	0.94	4.1**
5	3.24	1.01	3.32	0.99	0.8
6	2.92	0.98	2.83	0.79	1.0
7	2.82	0.89	2.55	0.75	3.0**

N=383
*Significant at .05 level
**Significant at .01 level

Based on the results of Student's t test which rendered a value of 2.03 (D.F.=383, $p/.04$) this null hypothesis was rejected. Rejecting the hypothesis means that there is a difference in the attitude toward amalgamation between Mexican Americans in the eighth grade in public schools and those in parochial schools.

Of the seven items which comprised the section, parochial school Mexican Americans had higher mean scores on five of them. The differences in responses between students from the two school systems were found to be significant on three items at the .003 level or beyond. Table 34, on the preceding page, presents a more complete and detailed resume of the results.

Controlling for Sex

Respondents of both sexes from parochial schools had higher means than those from public schools but only the difference between the females, with a t of 1.91, was significant at the .05 level. Table 35 shows that females in general had slightly higher means than males.

TABLE 35

COMPARISON OF ATTITUDE TOWARD AMALGAMATION BY SEX

Sex	Means Public	Parochial	t	D.F.	Prob.
Males	16.4	16.8	0.96	188	.34
Females	16.2	17.2	1.91*	195	.05
	Males	Females			
All Schools	16.6	16.7	0.27	383	.78

*Significant

Controlling for Religion

There was a significant difference between Catholics in public schools and those in parochial schools. The latter group showed a more favorable attitude toward amalgamation. It can be seen in Table 36 that the t value of 2.42 was significant at the .02 level. When all Catholics and non-Catholics were compared, regardless of school system, it was found that non-Catholics had a slightly higher means.

TABLE 36

COMPARISON OF ATTITUDE TOWARD AMALGAMATION BY RELIGION

Religion	Means Public	Parochial	t	D.F.	Prob.
Catholic	16.2	17.0	2.42*	357	.02
	Catholic	Non-Catholic			
All Schools	16.7	17.1	0.53	383	.60

*Significant

Controlling for Class

Both middle and working class respondents from parochial schools had higher means than those similarly classified in public schools. Table 37 shows that neither

59

comparison resulted in a significant difference, although one did reach the .08 level.

In the comparison between middle and working class, when school system was not controlled, it was found that the middle class had a significantly higher mean score. The difference resulted in a t of 3.00, which was significant at the .003 level. It should be noted that there was a direct relationship between SES and a favorable attitude toward amalgamation.

TABLE 37

COMPARISON OF ATTITUDE TOWARD AMALGAMATION BY CLASS

Class	Means Public	Parochial	t	D.F.	Prob.
Middle	16.5	17.9	1.72	119	.08
Working	16.3	16.5	0.53	244	.60
	Middle	Working			
All Schools	17.6	16.4	3.00*	363	.003

*Significant

Controlling for Religiosity

Table 38 reveals that public school respondents classified high had higher means than the parochial school respondents. A comparison of those classified medium,

TABLE 38

COMPARISON OF ATTITUDE TOWARD AMALGAMATION BY RELIGIOSITY

Religiosity	Means Public	Parochial	t	D.F.	Prob.
High	17.7	16.8	1.34	121	.18
Medium	15.8	17.1	2.76*	221	.006
	High	Medium			
All Schools	17.1	16.6	1.33	342	.18
	Medium	Low			
All Schools	16.6	15.8	1.71	262	.08

*Significant

however, favored those in parochial schools with a t value of 2.76. This reached the .006 level of significance. It can be seen that overall there was a direct relationship between religiosity and attitude toward amalgamation, with the high group having an advantage over the medium group and the medium group over the low in the comparisons which included the entire sample.

Controlling for Aspirational Level

In the inter-system comparisons parochial school respondents had higher means than public school respondents for all three categories. When making comparisons without regard for school system, it was revealed that there existed a direct relationship between AL and favorable attitude toward amalgamation. Refer to Table 39 for the complete results.

TABLE 39

COMPARISON OF ATTITUDE TOWARD AMALGAMATION
BY ASPIRATIONAL LEVEL

Aspirational Level	Means		t	D.F.	Prob.
	Public	Parochial			
High	16.4	17.1	1.68	231	.09
Medium	16.6	16.9	0.55	132	.59
Low	13.9	15.4	1.83	20	.08
	High	Medium			
All Schools	16.9	16.7	0.33	363	.74
	Medium	Low			
All Schools	16.7	14.5	4.01*	152	.0001

*Significant

As can be seen in the table, only one of the comparisons resulted in a significant difference. The medium AL group exhibited a much more favorable attitude than did the low group. The t value of 4.01 was significant beyond the .0001 level.

Controlling for School System Attendance Consistency

High and medium SSAC students from parochial schools exhibited higher means than their public school counterparts. Although the differences were not found to be significant at the .05 level, they did reach the .08 and .06 levels of significance. Table 40 also indicated that in a comparison within the public school system the high group had a higher mean score than the medium group, whereas in the parochial school

TABLE 40

COMPARISON OF ATTITUDE TOWARD AMALGAMATION
BY SCHOOL SYSTEM ATTENDANCE CONSISTENCY

SSAC	Means Public	Parochial	t	D.F.	Prob.
High	16.3	16.9	1.75	331	.08
Medium	15.9	18.2	1.93	29	.06
	High	Medium			
Public	16.3	15.9	0.43	165	.67
Parochial	16.9	18.2	1.56	195	.12
	Medium	Low			
Parochial	18.2	16.4	1.73	38	.09

*Significant

system the result was reversed. In parochial schools the medium group also showed higher means than the low group. Thus there was a direct relationship between SSAC and a favorable attitude toward amalgamation.

Controlling for Ethnic Composition School Type

Respondents from types 1 and 2 parochial schools enjoyed higher means than the similar type public schools. Only the difference between type 1 school groups was significant, with a t of 2.56. Table 41 shows that this was significant at the .01 level. In addition, four of the five items on which there was a significant difference were found to be so at the .01 level. Within the public school system the type 2 school respondents showed a significantly greater degree of favorableness toward amalgamation than those in type 1 schools. The t of 4.29 was significant at the .0001 level. Those from type 3 public schools were even more favorable than those in type 2 schools, and the t value of 2.68 was found to be significant at the .009 level.

In the parochial system the same inverse relationship between percent of Mexican American students and degree of favorableness toward amalgamation emerged. Thus type 2 school respondents had higher means than respondents from type 1 schools.

TABLE 41

COMPARISON OF ATTITUDE TOWARD AMALGAMATION
BY ETHNIC COMPOSITION SCHOOL TYPE

ECST	Means Public	Parochial	t	D.F.	Prob.
Type 1	15.2	16.8	2.56*	256	.01
Type 2	17.3	17.5	0.36	116	.71
	Type 1	Type 2			
Public	15.2	17.3	4.29*	157	.0001
Parochial	16.8	17.5	1.33	215	.18
	Type 2	Type 3			
Public	17.3	20.9	2.68*	68	.009

*Significant

Controlling for Parentage of Respondents

There was a significant difference, with a t value of 2.55, between the means of students attending public and parochial schools who had both a Mexican American mother and father. The difference, which favored those in parochial schools, was significant at the .01 level. Children of ethnically mixed marriages attending public schools once again exhibited higher means than their parochial school counterparts. See Table 42.

TABLE 42

COMPARISON OF ATTITUDE TOWARD AMALGAMATION
BY PARENTAGE OF RESPONDENTS

Parentage of Respondents	Means Public	Parochial	t	D.F.	Prob.
Both MA	16.0	16.8	2.55*	352	.01
MA Mother	20.4	19.1	0.83	23	.42
MA Father	20.5	18.8	0.57	8	.59

*Significant

63

Discussion

The data in this section indicate a difference in responses which favors parochial school respondents. It is this group of individuals who appear to have a more favorable attitude toward amalgamation. Although all of the control variables were introduced into the analysis, the results remained rather consistent.

Non-Catholics were slightly more inclined to accept amalgamation than were Catholics. This was possible due, at least in part, to the question regarding probability of marrying a WASP. As would be expected, non-Catholics are significantly more likely to answer in the affirmative since for them it does not mean marrying outside of the "one true faith" as it does for Catholics. Catholics are discouraged by their Church from entering inter-faith marriages which are looked upon as a possible threat to their own religious beliefs and practices. This question of Catholics marrying non-Catholics is discussed by Vernon (1962:324-37).

It is of interest to note that in public schools those high in SSAC showed a more favorable attitude toward amalgamation than those classified as medium. Thus, there exists a direct relationship between length of time attending a public school and favorable attitude toward amalgamation. In parochial schools, however, those medium in SSAC were more favorable, therefore revealing an inverse relationship. These two related findings are consistent and point to the same thing. Namely, the longer a student goes to a parochial school the more indoctrinated he becomes in Catholic beliefs and attitudes, both of which tend to discourage inter-faith or so-called "mixed marriages." This possible interpretation is weakened, however, by the fact that in parochial schools individuals classified as medium also exhibited a more favorable attitude towards amalgamation than did those classified as low. This is contrary to the expectations derived from the above discussion.

Hypothesis Five

There is no difference in the degree of identificational assimilation between eighth grade Mexican Americans in public schools and those in parochial schools.

This hypothesis was tested by means of the eleven different items which constituted Section III of the questionnaire. These items attempted to elicit the respondents' feelings and attitudes towards America and their degree of identification with her.

Based on the results of Student's t test this null hypothesis was also rejected. The t value was 2.04 (D.F.=383, $p/.04$). Thus, it cannot be said that Mexican Americans in both parochial and public schools are equal in their degree of identificational assimilation. The data indicated a significant and consistent difference in favor of respondents in public schools. In addition to a higher overall mean, public school respondents exhibited greater assimilation on seven of the items. Of the eleven items, there were significant differences between the two Mexican American groups on three of them. Refer to Table 43 for the complete results of Section III.

Controlling for Sex

Public school males and females had higher mean scores indicating a greater degree of identificational assimilation, than those in parochial schools.

TABLE 43

SECTION III COMPARISON OF RESULTS BY ITEM

Item	Public		Parochial		
	Mean	S.D.	Mean	S.D.	t
1	3.47	1.34	3.26	1.40	1.5
2	4.02	1.04	3.87	1.06	1.4
3	4.12	0.85	4.24	0.91	1.4
4	3.88	0.84	3.75	0.83	1.5
5	3.86	1.03	4.02	1.01	1.5
6	2.90	1.06	2.52	1.12	3.5*
7	3.50	1.08	3.60	1.13	0.9
8	3.96	0.87	4.03	0.89	0.8
9	3.02	1.29	2.59	1.24	3.3**
10	3.49	1.24	3.21	1.36	2.1*
11	2.71	1.14	2.53	1.16	1.5

N=383
*Significant at .05 level
**Significant at .01 level

Table 44 shows that in comparing the responses of all respondents of both sexes, without regard for the school system attended, females had higher means than males.

TABLE 44

COMPARISON OF IDENTIFICATIONAL ASSIMILATION BY SEX

Sex	Means		t	D.F.	Prob.
	Public	Parochial			
Male	38.8	37.5	1.26	188	.21
Female	39.1	37.8	1.70	1b5	.09
	Male	Female			
All Schools	38.0	38.4	0.55	383	.59

Controlling for Religion

Catholics from public schools showed a higher mean score than those from parochial schools. Unlike previous comparisons controlling for this variable, when all Catholics and non-Catholics were compared it was found that there was a significant difference in responses which favored the latter group.

As Table 45 reveals, non-Catholics enjoyed a significantly greater degree of identificational assimilation with a t value of 2.49, which was significant at the .01 level.

TABLE 45

COMPARISON OF IDENTIFICATIONAL ASSIMILATION BY RELIGION

	Means				
Religion	Public	Parochial	t	D.F.	Prob.
Catholic	38.5	37.6	1.38	357	.17
	Catholic	Non-Catholic			
All Schools	38.0	41.4	2.49*	383	.01

*Significant

Controlling for Class

Comparisons of respondents from both school systems showed that middle and working class students from public schools had higher means. The difference between middle class groups was significant at the .02 level, with a t value of 2.35. See Table 46 for more complete details. It should be noted that opposite results were obtained in the two school systems. Working class respondents showed higher means than middle class respondents when they were compared regardless of school system.

TABLE 46

COMPARISON OF IDENTIFICATIONAL ASSIMILATION BY CLASS

	Means				
Class	Public	Parochial	t	D.F.	Prob.
Middle	39.7	36.8	2.35*	119	.02
Working	38.8	38.3	0.60	244	.56
	Middle	Working			
All Schools	37.5	38.6	1.43	363	.15

*Significant

Controlling for Religiosity

Public school respondents in both high and medium RE categories exhibited higher means than those similarly classified in parochial schools. Table 47 reveals that the difference between the medium groups was significant with a t value of 1.97. This was significant at the .05 level. When respondents from both systems were combined and then compared on the basis of belonging to the high, medium or low categories. The results showed that there existed a direct relationship between religiosity and identificational assimilation, such that the higher the respondents were classified in RE the higher were their means.

TABLE 47

COMPARISON OF IDENTIFICATIONAL ASSIMILATION BY RELIGIOSITY

Religiosity	Means		t	D.F.	Prob.
	Public	Parochial			
High	40.3	38.2	1.69	121	.09
Medium	38.9	37.3	1.97*	221	.05
	High	Medium			
All Schools	39.0	37.9	1.41	342	.16
	Medium	Low			
All Schools	37.9	37.5	0.41	262	.68

*Significant

Controlling for Aspirational Level

All those groups, high, medium, and low composed of respondents attending public schools enjoyed higher means than the corresponding groups made up of those in parochial schools. Although neither difference was significant, one did reach the .09 level, as can be seen in Table 48. In comparing the different groups without controlling for school system, it was found that the high category exhibited a somewhat greater degree of identificational assimilation than the medium category, while this category, in turn, showed a slightly greater degree than the low. Thus, there was a direct relationship between aspiration and identificational assimilation.

TABLE 48

COMPARISON OF IDENTIFICATIONAL ASSIMILATION
BY ASPIRATIONAL LEVEL

Aspirational Level	Means Public	Parochial	t	D.F.	Prob.
High	39.2	37.8	1.69	231	.09
Medium	38.7	37.4	1.15	132	.25
Low	38.5	36.5	0.96	20	.35
	High	Medium			
All Schools	38.3	38.1	0.35	363	.73
	Medium	Low			
All Schools	38.1	37.7	0.33	152	.74

Controlling for School System Attendance Consistency

Respondents classified high and medium from public schools had higher means. The difference between the high public and parochial students was significant at the .05 level, with the t value being 1.99. Table 49 shows that intra-system comparisons revealed that in public schools high SSAC respondents had a slightly larger means than

TABLE 49

COMPARISON OF IDENTIFICATIONAL ASSIMILATION BY
SCHOOL SYSTEM ATTENDANCE CONSISTENCY

SSAC	Means Public	Parochial	t	D.F.	Prob.
High	39.0	37.8	1.99*	331	.05
Medium	38.6	37.8	0.33	29	.75
	High	Medium			
Public	39.0	38.6	0.24	165	.81
Parochial	37.8	37.8	0.01	195	.99
	Medium	Low			
Parochial	37.8	36.5	0.42	38	.68

*Significant

68

those classified medium, while in parochial schools there was virtually no difference whatsoever. However, medium SSAC students did have higher means than low students in parochial schools.

Controlling for Ethnic Composition School Type

Regardless of whether dealing with type 1 or type 2 schools, public school respondents showed greater identification with America than did parochial school respondents, as can be seen in Table 50. Within the public education system comparisons revealed an inverse relationship between ratio of Mexican Americans in the class and identificational assimilation. The difference between types 1 and 2 school respondents was significant at the .05 level. The value of t was 1.93.

TABLE 50

COMPARISON OF IDENTIFICATIONAL ASSIMILATION BY
ETHNIC COMPOSITION SCHOOL TYPE

ECST	Means Public	Parochial	t	D.F.	Prob.
Type 1	38.0	37.5	0.68	256	.45
Type 2	39.8	38.1	1.22	116	.20
	Type 1	Type 2			
Public	38.0	39.8	1.93*	157	.05
Parochial	37.5	38.1	0.49	215	.63
	Type 2	Type 3			
Public	39.8	42.9	1.67	68	.10

*Significant

In the parochial system the same inverse relationship was found to exist although the difference between the students was smaller.

Controlling for Parentage of Respondents

In keeping with the general reversal which was found when dealing with this subtype of assimilation from the previously consistent pattern which favored those from parochial schools, the comparison of respondents whose parents were both Mexican Americans revealed that public school respondents enjoyed higher means. Table 51 indicates that as in all such previous inter-system comparisons, Mexican American students in public schools with one Anglo parent showed a greater degree of assimilation. In this case, both of the differences were found to be very significant. The

TABLE 51

COMPARISON OF IDENTIFICATIONAL ASSIMILATION
BY PARENTAGE OF RESPONDENTS

Parentage of Respondents	Means Public	Parochial	t	D.F.	Prob.
Both MA	38.4	47.8	1.03	352	.30
MA Mother	45.0	37.3	2.82*	23	.01
MA Father	45.5	33.3	4.55*	8	.004

*Significant

t resulting from the comparison between those with MA mothers was 2.82, significant at the .01 level, and the t obtained in comparing those MA fathers was 4.55, significant at the .004 level.

Discussion

This was the one section in which the data indicated a complete reversal of the heretofore consistent advantage enjoyed by parochial school respondents. In contrast to the previously examined subtypes of assimilation, Mexican Americans in public schools showed a significantly greater degree of identificational assimilation. One of the reasons for this appears to be found in the degree of emphasis given to the individual's identity as an American in each of the school systems.

For anyone who has ever attended a parochial school it is immediately evident that a person's main identity is derived from his or her membership in the Church. This is what is taught and stressed. (Witness the great number of supporters enjoyed by Notre Dame teams from among Catholics all over the country). It is thus Church membership which unites all peoples, making them members of the same family, in which God is their Father and the Virgin Mary is their Mother. This identity cross-cuts every nationality, every race, and every time period. The recent Ecumenical Council Vatican II has reaffirmed this position (Abbott, 1966:14-37).

On the other hand, in public schools it is a person's citizenship and identity as an American which unites all members of the student body, as well as the community. While most classes in parochial schools begin with a prayer--now absent in public schools--more frequent recitation of the Pledge of Allegiance and the National Anthem are common in the public schools.

Consistent with this was the finding that no matter which control variable was introduced into the analysis, the difference favoring public school students failed to disappear or substantially diminish. Additional support came from the finding that non-Catholics showed greater identificational assimilation than Catholics regardless of the school attended.

Hypothesis Six

There is no difference between the attitude receptional assimilation (absence of prejudice) of eighth grade Mexican Americans in public schools and those in parochial schools.

This hypothesis was tested by means of eight separate items which were designed to indicate the respondents' feelings and attitudes towards different people. These items comprised Section V of the questionnaire.

Based on the results of Student's t, this null hypothesis was rejected, with a t value of 4.84 (D.F.=383, $p/.0001$). This means, therefore, that there is a very significant difference between the attitude receptional assimilation of eighth grade Mexican American students in public and parochial schools. Refer to Table 52 for the complete results.

TABLE 52

SECTION V COMPARISON OF RESULTS BY ITEM

| Item | Public | | Parochial | | t |
	Mean	S.D.	Mean	S.D.	
1	4.08	1.13	4.27	0.95	1.7
2	4.20	1.13	4.33	1.03	1.2
3	3.86	1.33	3.96	1.33	0.7
4	4.11	1.31	4.08	1.41	0.2
5	3.32	1.08	4.08	0.94	7.3**
6	4.07	1.02	4.25	0.84	1.8
7	3.77	1.15	4.33	0.75	5.4**
8	4.04	1.11	4.41	0.91	3.5**

N=383
*Significant at .05 level
**Significant at .01 level

As can be seen from the table, parochial school respondents showed greater assimilation on all but one of the items. Three of these differences in the responses between Mexican Americans from the two school systems were found to be significant at the .001 level or beyond.

Controlling for Sex

Parochial school males and females enjoyed significantly higher means than public school males. The t value obtained in the comparison between males was 4.01, which was significant beyond the .0001 level. For the comparison between females a t of 3.18 resulted which was significant at the .002 level. Table 53 shows that when comparing all males and females in the entire sample, females were significantly more assimilated than males. The t value of 2.68 which resulted from the comparison was significant at the .008 level.

TABLE 53

COMPARISON OF ATTITUDE RECEPTIONAL ASSIMILATION BY SEX

Sex	Means Public	Parochial	t	D.F.	Prob.
Male	30.6	33.2	4.01*	188	.0001
Female	32.2	34.3	3.18*	195	.002
	Male	Female			
All Schools	32.1	33.3	2.68*	383	.008

*Significant

Controlling for Religion

Catholics attending parochial schools showed a significantly greater degree of attitude receptional assimilation than those in public schools. The value of t was 5.03 which was found to be significant well beyond the .0001 level. Although the difference was relatively small, Catholics did have higher means than non-Catholics when they were compared without regard for the school system. Refer to Table 54 for complete results.

TABLE 54

COMPARISON OF ATTITUDE RECEPTIONAL ASSIMILATION BY RELIGION

Religion	Means Public	Parochial	t	D.F.	Prob.
Catholic	31.3	33.7	5.03*	357	.0001
	Catholic	Non-Catholic			
All Schools	32.8	32.4	0.35	383	.73

*Significant

Controlling for Class

Both middle and working class respondents from parochial schools exhibited higher means than their public school counterparts. The comparison between working class students yielded a t of 4.61. This was beyond the .0001 level of significance. Table 55 reveals that when all middle and working class respondents were compared, regardless of school attended, those in the middle class had a higher mean score. The resulting t value was 2.08, significant at the .04 level. It should be noted that there was a direct relationship found between class and absence of prejudice within the public school system as well as overall, but that it was not in the parochial system where students, regardless of class, showed less prejudice.

TABLE 55

COMPARISON OF ATTITUDE RECEPTIONAL ASSIMILATION BY CLASS

Class	Means Public	Parochial	t	D.F.	Prob.
Middle	32.7	33.7	1.09	119	.28
Working	31.2	33.8	4.61*	244	.0001
	Middle	Working			
All Schools	33.5	32.5	2.08*	363	.04

*Significant

Controlling for Religiosity

In Table 56 it can be seen that in comparisons the parochial school respondents enjoyed a nearly significant advantage over public school students classified high, and did have a significant advantage over those classified as medium. The latter

TABLE 56

COMPARISON OF ATTITUDE RECEPTIONAL ASSIMILATION BY RELIGIOSITY

Religiosity	Means Public	Parochial	t	D.F.	Prob.
High	32.2	33.7	1.83	121	.07
Medium	31.5	33.7	3.61*	221	.001
	High	Medium			
All Schools	33.1	32.9	0.55	342	.59
	Medium	Low			
All Schools	32.9	30.8	2.58*	262	.01

*Significant

73

value of t was 3.61, which reached the .001 level of significance. Comparisons which combined all respondents from both school systems revealed that an overall direct relationship prevailed between religiosity and attitude receptional assimilation. The difference between the medium and low groups was significant at the .01 level with a t-value of 2.58.

Controlling for Aspirational Level

There were significant differences between both the high and medium public school groups and the corresponding groups in parochial schools. In both cases the groups from the latter schools had the higher means. For the high groups the resulting t was 2.74, significant at the .007 level, while for the medium groups the t value which was obtained was 3.93. This value was significant at the .0001 level. When the low aspirational level groups were compared, however, the public school students held the advantage. Table 57 shows that when all respondents, regardless of school attended, were compared the results revealed the existence of a direct relationship between level of aspiration and attitude receptional assimilation, so that those of a higher category were more assimilated. The difference between the high and medium groups was significant at the .003 level with the t being 3.08.

TABLE 57

COMPARISON OF ATTITUDE RECEPTIONAL ASSIMILATION
BY ASPIRATIONAL LEVEL

Aspirational Level	Means Public	Parochial	t	D.F.	Prob.
High	32.4	34.0	2.74*	231	.007
Medium	30.4	33.5	3.93*	132	.0001
Low	31.0	29.8	0.70	20	.50
	High	Medium			
All Schools	33.4	31.8	3.08*	363	.003
	Medium	Low			
All Schools	31.8	30.5	1.44	152	.15

*Significant

Controlling for School System Attendance Consistency

Parochial school respondents had higher means than those from public schools in comparisons involving both high and medium SSAC categories. In the comparison involving the former groups a t value of 5.14 was obtained. This was well beyond the .0001 level of significance. Intra-system comparisons in public schools revealed that the respondents classified medium had higher means than those high. As can be seen in Table 58, the corresponding comparisons in the parochial system resulted in the same finding, although the difference was virtually non-existant. The medium group showed a greater degree of assimilation than the low group.

TABLE 58

COMPARISON OF ATTITUDE RECEPTIONAL ASSIMILATION BY
SCHOOL SYSTEM ATTENDANCE CONSISTENCY

SSAC	Means Public	Parochial	t	D.F.	Prob.
High	31.4	33.9	5.14*	331	.0001
Medium	32.5	33.9	0.82	29	.42
	High	Medium			
Public	31.4	32.5	0.72	165	.48
Parochial	33.9	33.9	0.03	195	.98
	Medium	Low			
Parochial	33.9	31.8	1.50	38	.14

*Significant

Controlling for Ethnic Composition School Type

Inter-system comparisons between respondents from the various corresponding school types indicated that parochial school students had higher mean assimilation scores. The difference between the type 1 school students, with a t value of 6.32, was significant well beyond the .0001 level. Table 59 reveals that between types 1 and 2 public schools there existed a significant difference which favored the latter. The t value of 4.78 was significant at the .0001 level. These respondents from type 2 schools were also found to have higher means than those from type 3 public schools.

In the parochial system, type 2 school respondents had higher means than type 1 school respondents. As can be seen, however, the difference was not significant.

TABLE 59

COMPARISON OF ATTITUDE RECEPTIONAL ASSIMILATION BY
ETHNIC COMPOSITION SCHOOL TYPE

ECST	Means Public	Parochial	t	D.F.	Prob.
Type 1	30.0	33.6	6.32*	256	.0001
Type 2	33.6	33.9	0.28	116	.70
	Type 1	Type 2			
Public	30.0	33.6	4.78*	157	.0001
Parochial	33.6	33.9	0.45	215	.66
	Type 2	Type 3			
Public	33.6	32.6	0.93	68	.36

*Significant

Controlling for Parentage of Respondents

A very significant t value of 5.04, which was beyond the .0001 level of significance, was obtained when respondents from endogamous marriages were compared. Parochial school students in this comparison therefore showed a much greater degree of attitude receptional assimilation. However, as indicated in Table 60, when comparing

TABLE 60

COMPARISON OF ATTITUDE RECEPTIONAL ASSIMILATION BY
PARENTAGE OF RESPONDENTS

Parentage of Respondents	Means Public	Parochial	t	D.F.	Prob.
Both MA	31.2	33.7	5.04*	352	.0001
MA Mother	34.4	34.5	0.04	23	.97
MA Father	34.8	32.5	2.43*	8	.05

*Significant

the means of respondents from exogamous marriages there was virtually no difference between students from the two school systems having MA mothers, but a significant advantage was held by public school students in the remaining comparison. The difference between those with MA fathers was significant at the .05 level with a t of 2.43.

Discussion

No matter which variables were controlled, with the exception of parentage of respondents, the results consistently favored the parochial school respondents. This indicated that they were more assimilated in terms of attitude receptional assimilation. Of the eighteen inter-system comparisons which were reported, parochial school respondents were higher on fifteen, and the differences between the means of the two groups were significant well beyond the .01 level on eleven of these.

There are two possible interpretations for this. Assuming the results were correct and truly reflect the attitudes of the respondents, they may be attributed to the emphasis placed on the brotherhood of men, referred to in the previous discussion, which is found in the parochial schools. In addition, an attempt is made to present Christ and the saints as both role models and reference group. To the extent that this is successful, it would be expected that students experience less prejudice.

On the other hand, if one questions the results in terms of their correspondence to the true attitudes of the respondents, they may be attributed to greater social pressures perceived by students in church-related schools to express a lack of prejudice. This is especially true while they are in the classroom or on the school premises.

Hypothesis Seven

There is no difference between the behavior receptional assimilation (absence of discrimination) of eighth grade Mexican Americans in public schools and those in parochial schools.

This hypothesis was tested, in Section IV, by means of eight items. Each of these items provides some measure of the discrimination which the respondents perceive. While this perceived discrimination may not reflect the reality of the situation, it does give an indication of the framework within which these students react and operate-- as explained by W. I. Thomas.

Based on the results of Student's t, which yielded a value of 5=0.27 (D.F.= 383, p/.79) the null hypothesis was not rejected. Therefore, we cannot say that there is any significant difference between the behavior receptional assimilation of the eighth grade Mexican American students in public and parochial schools.

A comparison by items reveals, however, that on five items the Mexican American students in public schools were closer to responses of the Anglos than were those in parochial schools. These latter Mexican Americans were closer to the Anglos on only three items. On three of the eight items the differences between Mexican Americans in parochial and those in public schools were found to be significant. See Table 61 for complete results.

TABLE 61

SECTION IV COMPARISON OF RESULTS BY ITEM

Item	Public Mean	S.D.	Parochial Mean	S.D.	t
1	3.59	1.08	3.57	1.17	0.2
2	3.44	1.18	3.67	1.15	1.9*
3	3.10	1.30	3.32	1.38	1.6
4	3.17	1.17	2.76	1.23	3.3**
5	3.62	1.12	3.86	1.09	2.1*
6	3.48	1.13	3.45	1.27	0.2
7	3.67	1.00	3.65	1.03	0.2
8	3.16	1.19	3.09	1.10	0.6

N=383
*Significant at .05 level
**Significant at .01 level

Controlling for Sex

Males and females from parochial schools had higher means than their public school counterparts but in both cases the differences were slight. Table 62 shows that the difference between all respondents of both sexes favored the females. This difference approached but did not reach the acceptable significance level.

TABLE 62

COMPARISON OF BEHAVIOR RECEPTIONAL ASSIMILATION BY SEX

Sex	Means Public	Parochial	t	D.F.	Prob.
Male	26.8	26.9	0.12	188	.90
Female	27.6	27.9	0.41	195	.68

	Male	Female			
All Schools	26.8	27.8	1.78	383	.07

Controlling for Religion

There was virtually no difference between the means of Catholics in public and parochial schools, as is apparent in Table 63. In the comparison between all

TABLE 63

COMPARISON OF BEHAVIOR RECEPTIONAL ASSIMILATION BY RELIGION

Religion	Means Public	Parochial	t	D.F.	Prob.
Catholic	27.4	27.4	0.01	357	.99
	Catholic	Non-Catholic			
All Schools	27.4	26.2	0.98	383	.33

Catholics and non-Catholics, without controlling for school system, it was found that Catholics had a higher mean score than non-Catholics.

Controlling for Class

Middle class public school respondents showed a significantly greater degree of behavior receptional assimilation than those in public schools. The value of t was 3.73, which was significant at the .001 level. Among the working class, however, it was the parochial school students who were significantly more assimilated. Table 64 reveals that the t value of 2.20 was significant at the .03 level.

Comparing the means of middle and working class respondents, regardless of school attended, it was shown that there was a direct relationship between class and absence of discrimination. This relationship obtained in the public system as well, but not in the parochial system.

TABLE 64

COMPARISON OF BEHAVIOR RECEPTIONAL ASSIMILATION BY CLASS

Class	Means Public	Parochial	t	D.F.	Prob.
Middle	30.6	26.7	3.73*	119	.001
Working	26.4	27.9	2.20*	244	.03
	Middle	Working			
All Schools	27.7	27.1	0.94	363	.35

*Significant

Controlling for Religiosity

The comparison of respondents classified high indicated that public school students had slightly larger means. Among students classified medium, it was also those in public schools who enjoyed a higher mean score. It can be seen in Table 65 that when the high and medium groups were compared, combining the two school systems, the former group had the higher means. When the medium and low groups were similarly compared, the medium group was shown to be significantly more assimilated. The resulting t value was 3.78 which was significant at the .0001 level. Thus, there resulted within each system, as well as overall, a direct relationship between religiosity and behavior receptional assimilation.

TABLE 65

COMPARISON OF BEHAVIOR RECEPTIONAL ASSIMILATION BY RELIGIOSITY

Religiosity	Means Public	Parochial	t	D.F.	Prob.
High	28.1	27.6	0.39	121	.70
Medium	27.9	27.2	0.98	221	.33
	High	Medium			
All Schools	27.8	27.5	0.53	342	.60
	Medium	Low			
All Schools	27.5	24.9	3.78*	262	.0001

*Significant

Controlling for Aspirational Level

Table 66 shows that while public school respondents classified high had larger means, in the comparisons involving those classified medium and low it was the parochial school students who enjoyed the advantage.

Inter-category comparisons involving the entire sample revealed the existence of a direct relationship between aspirational level and behavior receptional assimilation. The difference between the high and medium groups resulted in a t of 2.84, significant at the .005 level. This same direct relationship can also be observed within both systems.

TABLE 66

COMPARISON OF BEHAVIOR RECEPTIONAL ASSIMILATION BY ASPIRATIONAL LEVEL

Aspirational Level	Means Public	Parochial	t	D.F.	Prob.
High	28.4	27.7	0.99	231	.32
Medium	26.1	26.7	0.76	132	.46
Low	25.3	25.6	0.18	20	.85
	High	Medium			
All Schools	28.0	26.4	2.84*	363	.005
	Medium	Low			
All Schools	26.4	25.4	0.97	152	.34

*Significant

Controlling for School System Attendance Consistency

Once again the results neither consistently favored one system nor reached the significance level. Comparing the means of the two high groups showed that parochial school students had larger means, but when the two medium groups were compared it was the respondents from public schools who had higher means.

Comparisons within the public school system between the high and medium groups revealed that the medium group was somewhat more assimilated. From Table 67 it can be seen that the same comparison in the parochial school system showed the high group to have the larger mean score. When comparing the medium with the low group it was found that there was almost no difference between them. However, it may be noted that, although not very strong, there was a direct relationship between SSAC and behavior receptional assimilation in the parochial schools.

Controlling for Ethnic Composition School Type

Parochial school respondents attending type 1 schools enjoyed significantly higher means than their counterparts in public schools. The t value of 2.03 was significant at the .05 level. A similar comparison involving those from type 2 schools showed the public school students to have the higher means. Table 68 gives the complete results obtained.

Inter-system comparisons between respondents in types 1 and 2 public schools favored those in type 2 schools. The difference yielded a t value of 2.47 which reached the .01 level of significance. When respondents from types 2 and 3 schools were compared it was again those from the type 2 schools who showed a greater degree of assimilation. The comparison between types 1 and 2 parochial school respondents showed that those in the type 1 schools had higher means.

TABLE 67

COMPARISON OF BEHAVIOR RECEPTIONAL ASSIMILATION
BY SCHOOL SYSTEM ATTENDANCE CONSISTENCY

SSAC	Means Public	Parochial	t	D.F.	Prob.
High	27.0	27.6	1.02	331	.31
Medium	28.7	26.4	1.27	29	.21
	High	Medium			
Public	27.0	28.7	1.09	165	.28
Parochial	27.6	26.4	1.09	215	.28
	Medium	Low			
Parochial	26.4	26.3	0.08	38	.94

TABLE 68

COMPARISON OF BEHAVIOR RECEPTIONAL ASSIMILATION
BY ETHNIC COMPOSITION SCHOOL TYPE

ECST	Means Public	Parochial	t	D.F.	Prob.
Type 1	26.4	27.7	2.03*	256	.05
Type 2	28.4	26.5	1.86	116	.07
	Type 1	Type 2			
Public	26.4	28.4	2.47*	157	.01
Parochial	27.7	26.5	1.37	215	.17
	Type 2	Type 3			
Public	28.4	27.8	0.39	68	.70

*Significant

82

Controlling for Parentage of Respondents

Comparing the means of students of both systems who had a Mexican American mother and father revealed that those in parochial schools appeared to be more assimilated. However, the comparisons involving students with one Anglo parent showed that once again it was the public school students who had higher means. Table 69 indicated that it did not matter whether the Anglo parent was the mother or the father.

TABLE 69

COMPARISON OF BEHAVIOR RECEPTIONAL ASSIMILATION
BY PARENTAGE OF RESPONDENTS

Parentage of Respondents	Means Public	Parochial	t	D.F.	Prob.
Both MA	27.0	27.4	0.65	352	.52
MA Mother	28.1	25.9	0.87	23	.40
MA Father	32.3	30.8	0.35	8	.73

Discussion

This was the only null hypothesis which was not rejected. Perhaps the most salient feature of the data just presented is the almost complete absence of statistically significant differences between public and parochial school Mexican Americans in the area of behavior receptional assimilation. No matter which control variable was introduced into the analysis, the two groups remained surprisingly alike in the degree of assimilation indicated.

This finding is really not surprising when one considers the fact that this aspect, or subtype, of assimilation, perhaps more than any other, depends not on the minority group but on the dominant group. While every type of assimilation depends on both internal forces, within the individual, and external forces found in society, that type dealing with discrimination is largely determined by the external forces (Schermerhorn, 1970).

When society, or a portion of society, discriminates against a minority group it is not really important what school a particular minority group member attends. The discrimination is not directed against a person as an individual, but as a member of a group, and the school one attends does not change that membership. Blumer explains how both prejudice and discrimination are based on group membership (1961:217-28; 1955).

The difficulty with being behavior receptionally assimilated, therefore, is not merely an individual matter, and, apparently, the school one attends does not really matter. Some light is shed on this by Jack Forbes (1970:15) who wrote:

Mexican-Americans are, therefore, a racial as well as a cultural
minority and the racial differences which set them apart from
Anglos cannot be made to "disappear" by any "Americanization"

process carried on in the schools.

Hypothesis Eight

There is no difference in the degree of civic assimilation between
the eighth grade Mexican Americans in the public schools and those
in parochial schools.

This hypothesis was tested by means of twelve different items; each item
questioned the respondents about their attitudes toward a law, obligation or civic
responsibility, as currently recognized in American society.

Based on the results of Student's t test, this null hypothesis was also rejected. The t value was 4.57 (D.F.=383, p/.0001). Therefore, there is a very significant difference between the degree of civic assimilation of the Mexican American public
school students and those in the parochial schools. Once again, it was those in the
church-related schools who were the most assimilated. Refer to Table 70 for the complete results of Section II.

Table 70 indicates that the Mexican Americans in parochial schools were more
similar to the Anglos on nine of the items while the Mexican Americans in public
schools were more similar on only two items. On one item there was no difference in
means between Mexican American groups. When comparing the means of the two groups on
the twelve items, six were significant at the .05 level or beyond.

TABLE 70

SECTION II COMPARISON OF RESULTS BY ITEM

Item	Public Mean	S.D.	Parochial Mean	S.D.	t
1	3.41	1.32	3.69	1.24	2.1*
2	3.71	1.05	3.95	0.92	2.3*
3	3.12	1.18	2.96	1.27	1.2
4	3.17	1.11	3.01	1.17	1.3
5	3.30	1.08	3.79	1.02	4.5**
6	2.93	1.06	3.31	0.96	3.6**
7	3.65	1.21	3.81	1.17	1.3
8	3.04	1.06	3.60	0.98	5.3**
9	4.08	0.87	4.18	0.85	1.1
10	3.35	1.23	3.35	1.27	0.1
11	3.79	1.11	3.98	0.98	1.7
12	4.26	1.10	4.61	0.86	3.4**

N=383
*Significant at .05 level
**Significant at .01 level

Controlling for Sex

A comparison of the means of respondents by sex revealed that parochial school students of both sexes showed a significantly greater degree of civic assimilation. The difference between males from the two school systems yielded a t value of 3.91 which was significant at the .0001 level. Between females the resulting t was 2.38 which reached the .02 level of significance as can be seen in Table 71.

When all males were compared with all females, regardless of school system, the latter respondents were found to have slightly higher means.

TABLE 71

COMPARISON OF CIVIC ASSIMILATION BY SEX

Sex	Means Public	Parochial	t	D.F.	Prob.
Male	41.1	44.6	3.91*	188	.0001
Female	42.4	43.9	2.38*	195	.02
	Male	Female			
All Schools	43.1	43.2	0.21	383	.83

*Significant

Controlling for Religion

There was a very significant difference between the means of public and parochial school Catholics. The latter exhibited a much greater degree of assimilation. A t value of 4.34, significant beyond the .0001 level, resulted from the comparison of the two groups. In a comparison between all Catholics and non-Catholics from both school systems, it was found that Catholics had a higher mean score. See Table 72 for

TABLE 72

COMPARISON OF CIVIC ASSIMILATION BY RELIGION

Religion	Means Public	Parochial	t	D.F.	Prob.
Catholic	42.1	44.2	4.34*	357	.0001
	Catholic	Non-Catholic			
All Schools	43.4	40.5	1.54	383	.12

*Significant

the complete results of the comparisons.

Controlling for Class

Middle and working class parochial schools respondents enjoyed higher means than their counterparts from public schools. The difference between working class students was significant at the .001 level with a t value of 3.54. Table 73 shows that when all middle and working class respondents were compared, regardless of the school attended, the results indicated that the former were significantly more assimilated. The t value of 3.84 was significant at the .0001 level. Therefore, overall as well as in both school systems, there was a direct relationship between SES and civic assimilation.

TABLE 73

COMPARISON OF CIVIC ASSIMILATION BY CLASS

Class	Means Public	Parochial	t	D.F.	Prob.
Middle	43.3	44.8	1.56	119	.12
Working	41.3	43.7	3.54*	244	.001
	Middle	Working			
All Schools	44.5	42.5	3.84*	363	.0001

*Significant

Controlling for Religiosity

Parochial school respondents who were classified high and medium showed a greater degree of assimilation than those similarly classified in public schools. The difference in means between the medium RE groups was significant at the .001 level with a t value of 3.45. It can be seen in Table 74 that the inter-category comparisons which combined all students from both systems revealed that a direct relationship exists between religiosity and civic assimilation. The difference between the medium and low groups was significant at the .003 level with the comparison yielding a t of 3.00. Within each school system this same direct relationship can be observed.

TABLE 74

COMPARISON OF CIVIC ASSIMILATION BY RELIGIOSITY

Religiosity	Means Public	Parochial	t	D.F.	Prob.
High	43.0	44.4	1.43	121	.15
Medium	41.5	44.2	3.45*	221	.001
	High	Medium			
All Schools	43.9	43.2	1.28	342	.20
	Medium	Low			
All Schools	43.2	40.9	3.00*	262	.003

*Significant

Controlling for Aspirational Level

Respondents in all three categories, high, medium and low, from parochial schools had higher means than those from public schools, and in two of the three comparisons the difference was very significant. The comparison between high groups yielded a t value of 2.71 which was significant at the .007 level. A t of 2.97, significant at the .004 level, resulted from the comparison of the medium groups.

TABLE 75

COMPARISON OF CIVIC ASSIMILATION BY ASPIRATIONAL LEVEL

Aspirational Level	Means Public	Parochial	t	D.F.	Prob.
High	42.8	44.5	2.71*	231	.007
Medium	41.0	43.9	2.97*	132	.004
Low	39.5	42.9	1.88	20	.07
	High	Medium			
All Schools	43.8	42.4	2.45*	363	.01
	Medium	Low			
All Schools	42.4	40.8	1.34	152	.18

*Significant

The data presented in Table 75 indicate that, as was the case within both school systems, there was a direct relationship between aspiration and civic assimilation found to obtain when inter-category comparisons involving all respondents were made. The difference between the high and medium groups was significant at the .01 level with a t value of 2.45.

TABLE 75

COMPARISON OF CIVIC ASSIMILATION BY ASPIRATIONAL LEVEL

Aspirational Level	Means Public	Parochial	t	D.F.	Prob.
High	42.8	44.5	2.71*	231	.007
Medium	41.0	43.9	2.97*	132	.004
Low	39.5	42.9	1.88	20	.07
	High	Medium			
All Schools	43.8	42.4	2.45*	363	.01
	Medium	Low			
All Schools	42.4	40.8	1.34	152	.18

*Significant

Controlling for School System Attendance Consistency

Parochial school respondents, both high and medium SSAC, showed a significantly greater degree of civic assimilation that their public school counterparts. Table 76 reveals that when the high groups were compared, a t of 4.43, significant beyond the .0001 level, was obtained.

The comparison of means of the medium groups resulted in a t value of 2.93 which reached the .007 level of significance.

A comparison within the public system between high and medium students yielded a significant t of 2.35, which was found to reach the .02 level. Comparisons within the parochial school system, as in public schools, indicated a direct relationship, so that the higher the category the greater the degree of assimilation.

Controlling for Ethnic Composition School Type

Comparing type 1 public and parochial school respondents resulted in an extremely large t value of 6.14 which, as Table 77 shows, was significant well beyond the .0001 level. In addition, on seven of the twelve items which composed the section, differences between the respondents were significant at .01. In the comparison involving respondents from type 2 schools it was those from public schools who had

TABLE 76

COMPARISON OF CIVIC ASSIMILATION BY SCHOOL SYSTEM
ATTENDANCE CONSISTENCY

	Means		t	D.F.	Prob.
SSAC	Public	Parochial			
High	42.0	44.5	4.43*	331	.0001
Medium	39.1	43.8	2.93*	29	.007
	High	Medium			
Public	42.0	39.1	2.35*	165	.02
Parochial	44.5	43.8	0.61	195	.55
	Medium	Low			
Parochial	43.8	42.5	0.86	38	.40

*Significant

had somewhat higher means.

Inter-system comparisons revealed that there existed an inverse relationship in the public system but a direct relationship between SSAC and civic assimilation in

TABLE 77

COMPARISON OF CIVIC ASSIMILATION BY ETHNIC
COMPOSITION SCHOOL TYPE

	Means		t	D.F.	Prob.
ECST	Public	Parochial			
Type 1	40.3	44.6	6.14	256	.0001
Type 2	43.8	43.2	0.69	116	.48
	Type 1	Type 2			
Public	40.3	43.8	4.17*	157	.0001
Parochial	44.6	43.2	2.03*	215	.04
	Type 2	Type 3			
Public	43.8	45.6	1.02	68	.31

*Significant

the parochial school system. Between types 1 and 2 public schools the difference was significant beyond the .0001 level, based on a t value of 4.17. The opposite results were obtained when the same comparison was made in the parochial system, where type 1 school respondents showed greater assimilation. A t value of 2.03 resulted from the comparison, and this was found to be significant at the .04 level.

Controlling for Parentage of Respondents

Students from endogamous marriages attending public and parochial schools were compared, and the results indicated that there was a significant difference between them which favored parochial school respondents. The resulting t value of 5.42 was beyond the .0001 level of significance. In addition to this, the differences on seven of the items were significant. Refer to Table 78 for the complete results.

TABLE 78

COMPARISON OF CIVIC ASSIMILATION
BY PARENTAGE OF RESPONDENTS

Parentage of Respondents	Means		t	D.F.	Prob.
	Public	Parochial			
Both MA	41.4	44.3	5.42*	352	.0001
MA Mother	47.4	43.6	2.26*	23	.03
MA Father	46.5	43.0	0.88	8	.42

*Significant

When comparisons were made involving those from exogamous marriages the data showed that as was the case on all previous hypotheses tested public school respondents exhibited greater assimilation. The comparison between students with a Mexican American mother was significant at the .03 level based on a t value of 2.26.

Discussion

The above data indicated that there was a significant difference in the degree of civic assimilation between public and parochial school Mexican Americans. As was true for all but one of the subtypes, it was those in the church-related schools who were more assimilated.

These findings are consistent with those of Lenski who found that Catholics, regardless of class, place a higher value on obedience than do non-Catholics (1967: 217-36). He also found that among middle class Catholics attendance at Catholic schools was linked with a greater appreciation of the value of obedience and less appreciation of the value of intellectual autonomy. In general, he found

    . . . those Catholics who have received all or most of their
    education in Catholic institutions are more faithful in their

observance of Catholic norms than those who received all or most
of their education in non-Catholic institutions (1967:228).

In addition, Lenski also noted that those who have attended Catholic schools are more
likely to vote than those who attended non-Catholic schools.

These elements, namely, obedience to laws and voting, are very important aspects of a person's civic responsibility, and are among the considerations involved in civic assimilation. The reason that these are promoted and fostered by a parochial school education is to be found in the importance obedience and law play in the practice of religion itself (Vernon, 1962:51-53). Voting and taking an active interest in government affairs, as well as fulfilling all civic responsibilities, are taught to be part of the Catholic's moral obligations.

Looking at it pragmatically, taking an active role in civic matters is one way to insure a group's rights and protect its self-interest. Since parochial schools are not in the same favored and protected position as public schools, Catholic school teachers and administrators might be expected to more actively encourage their students to become good, active citizens in order to ensure the future welfare of the parochial school system.

CHAPTER V

SUMMARY AND CONCLUSIONS

Assimilation refers to a process which basically tends to make a socially homogeneous group out of one that was heterogeneous. This concept has been used often, and has been understood and defined in numerous ways. For the present research, the explanation and framework provided by Milton Gordon was adopted. As such, assimilation was seen to involve seven basic subprocesses each of which may be thought of as constituting a particular stage or aspect of the assimilation process. Not only is the entire assimilation process a matter of degree but each of the subtypes or stages may likewise take place in varying degrees. Utilizing this framework, an attempt has been made in the present study to examine the relationship between the school system attended by Mexican Americans and their degree of assimilation.

The major findings of this research are as follows:

1. There is a significant difference in the degree of overall assimilation between eighth grade Mexican Americans in public schools and those in parochial schools.

   a. There is a significant difference in the degree of acculturation between the two groups.

   b. There is a significant difference in the degree of structural assimilation between the two groups.

   c. There is a significant difference in the attitude toward amalgamation between the two groups.

   d. There is a significant difference in the degree of identificational assimilation between the two groups.

   e. There is a significant difference in the degree of attitude receptional assimilation found in the two groups.

   f. There is a significant difference in the degree of civic assimilation between the two groups.

2. Those in parochial schools are significantly more assimilated in all of the above subtypes except identificational assimilation.

3. Those in public schools show a significantly greater degree of identificational assimilation.

4. There is no difference between behavior receptional assimilation (absence of discrimination) of eighth grade Mexican Americans in public schools and those in parochial schools.

5. Females are more assimilated than males.

6. Catholics are more assimilated than non-Catholics.

7. Middle class are more assimilated than working class.

8. There is a direct relationship between degree of RE and assimilation.

9. There is a direct relationship between degree of AL and assimilation.

10. In parochial schools there is a direct relationship between SSAC and assimilation.

11. There is a direct relationship between the percentage of Anglos in a school class and the assimilation of its Mexican American members.

12. Mexican Americans with one Anglo parent are more assimilated in public schools than in parochial schools.

The data revealed such a consistent pattern in favor of the parochial schools and the differences were of such magnitude that there can be little doubt about the existence of a relationship between school system attended and degree of assimilation. No matter which of the eight test factors were controlled, the difference failed to disappear.

It has been suggested in the discussions that this difference, which favors the church-related schools, has its locus in a self-selection process which is inherent in any private school. Concomitant with this self-selection is a greater commitment on the part of the school to meet the individual needs of its students and thereby develop their capabilities to the fullest. An important aspect of this development centers around religious training. As Herberg has indicated, however, in the United States religion has become Americanized to such a degree that as the parochial schools are making their students better Catholics they are at the same time making them better Americans.

Within the limits imposed by the population, sample, and methodology of this research, the findings suggest several important implications:

First of all, the findings imply that Gordon's theoretical framework for the study of assimilation can be fruitfully applied in the study of minority groups. Each of the subtypes do, in fact, appear to measure a separate aspect of assimilation, and they may vary independently of each other.

Second, the findings imply that there are indeed significant differences between the degree of assimilation, in all but one of the various subtypes herein investigated, of eighth grade Mexican Americans in public schools and those in parochial schools. It appears that with the sole exception of the area of identificational assimilation, the Mexican Americans in parochial schools are more assimilated, and hence more like the Anglo students. It is, therefore, a possibility that it is the parochial school system, which the government refuses to subsidize in any form even to the point of letting it collapse, which is more effective in "Americanizing" minority group members.

Third, the findings imply that the school system attended does not appreciably alter the discrimination experienced, or at least perceived, by the minority group members.

Finally, this study demonstrates the need for additional explanatory and replicative studies to further refine, extend, and clarify the limited knowledge which exists concerning the relationship between school system and assimilation. The role the school plays in the assimilation, or lack of it, of minority groups members should be examined in greater detail. Specifically, it is recommended that other student minority groups be studied, and that private schools other than Catholic be included.

APPENDIX A

SELECTION OF ITEMS

Section I

t= 4.44   1. A person's first responsibility is to his or her family.

t= 5.88   2. It's best not to be too friendly with your neighbors.

t= 2.77   3. A man should ignore an insult.

t= 2.95   4. A younger brother or sister should respect and obey an older brother.

t= 9.10   5. Making plans only brings unhappiness because they are hard to fulfill.

t= 4.00   6. With things as they are today an intelligent person ought to think only about the present, without worrying about what is going to happen tomorrow.

t= 6.41   7. The secret of happiness is not expecting too much out of life and being content with what comes your way.

t= 2.91   8. It is important to have good manners.

t=   .84* 9. Men should not have more freedom than women.

t= 2.79 10. A women's place is in the home.

t= 4.55 11. It is best if a person can always live near his parents.

t= 1.09* 12. It is better to hire a relative than a stranger for a job.

t=   .11* 13. A brother should protect a sister, even if she doesn't want help.

t= 1.77 14. It's better to be able to talk your way out of trouble than fight your way out.

t= 5.95 15. It's preferable to have just a few good friends than many people with whom you're friendly.

t= 7.75 16. To be a success it's necessary to be well educated.

t= 3.10 17. Neighbors often cause one harm.

t= 4.82 18. Women should respect and obey men.

t=   .87* 19. Education is something good and desirable, even if it doesn't help in getting a better job.

t= 2.09 20. It's better not to try something than it is to try and fail.

Section II

t=   4.82   1. There should be a limit placed on the number of children a family has.

t=   3.35   2. A family with five children is too big.

t=   2.56   3. Divorce should not be allowed.

t=   .61*   4. The laws should not allow abortion.

t=   1.77   5. Any married person should get a divorce if he or she so desires.

t=   4.38   6. Loyalty to the Church comes before loyalty to the government.

t=   2.79   7. If a state or federal law contradicts a church law, you should follow the state or federal law.

t=   1.88   8. A pregnancy should never be ended on purpose.

t=   3.70   9. It is more important to be a good citizen than a good church member.

t=   4.75   10. Every citizen should obey the laws of the country.

t=   2.19   11. No man should refuse to enter the military service when drafted.

t=   3.31   12. Everyone that is eligible should vote.

t=   2.69   13. No one should be kept from holding a public office because of race, creed or color.

Section III

t=   8.58   1. I just want to be called an American and nothing else, regarding nationality.

t=   8.88   2. I consider myself to be just as American as anyone else.

t= 11.55   3. I am proud to be called an American.

t=   6.93   4. I identify with America.

t=   1.11*   5. I am not just an American, but am a special kind of American.

t=   9.83   6. I do not think of myself as an American.

t=   4.03   7. I feel that I am one with all white Anglo-Saxon Protestants in the United States.

t=   4.56   8. When foreigners insult Americans they are insulting me.

t=   4.71   9. The celebrations of America are my celebrations.

t=   6.32   10. I do not feel a close relationship with any other country except the United States.

t= 4.53   11. In the international competitions (i.e., Olympics) I always root for the United States to beat every other nation.

t= 3.93   12. I feel almost as close (or closer) a relationship with Mexico as with the United States.

Section IV

t= 4.21   1. The other students treat me like everyone else.

t= 7.13   2. I have never been rejected by anyone because of my nationality.

t= 11.39   3. No one has ever made fun of me or called me names because of my nationality or ancestors.

t= 2.79   4. There is no discrimination in San Antonio against people of my nationality or ancestry.

t= 4.96   5. My nationality has caused me problems.

t= 3.80   6. I am invited to as many parties as the rest of my classmates.

t= 5.00   7. In this city I am treated as well as anyone else.

t= 1.77   8. There is some discrimination against people of my religion here in San Antonio.

t= 1.11*   9. In general people of dark skins (besides Blacks) are not treated as equals with whites in San Antonio.

Section V+

t= 4.58   5. People who go to public schools are usually better Americans than those who go to private schools.

t= 5.50   6. People who live in the United States should speak English all the time and not use some foreign language.

t= 4.50   7. I don't like people who go to private schools.

t= 4.30   8. A dark skinned person should not try to mix socially with whites.

Section VI+

t= 2.20   4. It's best for a person to date only those who are of the same nationality as he or she is.

t= 4.59   5. I will not restrict my selection of a spouse to one of my own nationality.

t= 6.65   6. I would like to marry an Anglo.

t= 4.73   7. I will probably marry a white Anglo Protestant.

t= 1.30*   8. I would not want to marry anyone with skin color different from mine.

*Item not utilized on final instrument because of insufficient t value.

+Only items which required agreement or disagreement with statements were included. Missing numbers indicate questions which were of the listing or ranking type.

APPENDIX B

PLEASE CHECK (X) THE APPROPRIATE SPACE

School: Public _____

      Parochial _____

Sex: Male _____

    Female _____

Religion:

Catholic _____

Protestant _____

Other _____

Ethnic Background
of Father   of Mother

_____ Anglo _____

_____ Mexican American _____

_____ Oriental _____

_____ Negro _____

(Please write - even if dead, retired or unemployed)

Occupation of Father _____

Occupation of Mother _____

Frequency of church attendance: at least once a week _____

                " a month _____

                " a year _____

                less often _____

Family prayer: daily _____

        weekly _____

      infrequently _____

         never _____

Bible reading: daily _____

        weekly _____

      infrequently _____

         never _____

Have you received religious instruction (such as Sunday School or CCD class) within the past year?
                Yes _____   No _____

Do you receive any religious training at home? Yes _____ No _____

Do you want to attend college? Yes _____ No _____

What do you want to be, or what career do you want to pursue, when you are older?

_____

How many years have you attended a public school? _____ years.

              a parochial school? _____ years.

PLEASE READ EACH STATEMENT CAREFULLY. DO NOT LOOK FOR HIDDEN MEANINGS, OR TRY TO GIVE AN ANSWER YOU THINK WE WANT OR YOU THINK YOU SHOULD GIVE.

CIRCLE THE ONE ANSWER UNDER EACH STATEMENT THAT COMES NEAREST TO YOUR TRUE FEELINGS IN RESPONDING TO THE STATEMENT.

PLEASE DO NOT LEAVE ANYTHING BLANK.

Section I

1. A person's first responsibility is to his or her family.
   strongly agree - agree - undecided - disagree - strongly disagree

2. It's best not to be too friendly with your neighbors.
   strongly agree - agree - undecided - disagree - strongly disagree

3. A man should ignore an insult.
   strongly agree - agree - undecided - disagree - strongly disagree

4. A younger brother or sister should respect and obey an older brother.
   strongly agree - agree - undecided - disagree - strongly disagree

5. Making plans only brings unhappiness because they are hard to fulfill.
   strongly agree - agree - undecided - disagree - strongly disagree

6. With things as they are today an intelligent person ought to think only about the present, without worrying about what is going to happen tomorrow.
   strongly agree - agree - undecided - disagree - strongly disagree

7. The secret of happiness is not expecting too much out of life and being content with what comes your way.
   strongly agree - agree - undecided - disagree - strongly disagree

8. It is important to have good manners.
   strongly agree - agree - undecided - disagree - strongly disagree

9. A woman's place is in the home.
   strongly agree - agree - undecided - disagree - strongly disagree

10. It is best if a person can always live near his parents.
    strongly agree - agree - undecided - disagree - strongly disagree

11. It's better to be able to talk your way out of trouble than fight your way out.
    strongly agree - agree - undecided - disagree - strongly disagree

12. It's preferable to have just a few good friends than many people with whom you are friendly.
    strongly agree - agree - undecided - disagree - strongly disagree

13. To be a success it's necessary to be well educated.
    strongly agree - agree - undecided - disagree - strongly disagree

14. Neighbors often cause one harm.
    strongly agree - agree - undecided - disagree - strongly disagree

15. Women should respect and obey men.
    strongly agree - agree - undecided - disagree - strongly disagree

16. It's better not to try something than it is to try and fail.
strongly agree - agree - undecided - disagree - strongly disagree

Section II

1. There should be a limit placed on the number of children a family has.
strongly agree - agree - undecided - disagree - strongly disagree

2. A family with five children is too big.
strongly agree - agree - undecided - disagree - strongly disagree

3. Divorce should not be allowed.
strongly agree - agree - undecided - disagree - strongly disagree

4. Any married person should get a divorce if he or she so desires.
strongly agree - agree - undecided - disagree - strongly disagree

5. Loyalty to the Church comes before loyalty to the government.
strongly agree - agree - undecided - disagree - strongly disagree

6. If a state or federal law contradicts a church law, you should follow the state or federal law.
strongly agree - agree - undecided - disagree - strongly disagree

7. A pregnancy should never be ended on purpose.
strongly agree - agree - undecided - disagree - strongly disagree

8. It is more important to be a good citizen than a good church member.
strongly agree - agree - undecided - disagree - strongly disagree

9. Every citizen should obey the laws of the country.
strongly agree - agree - undecided - disagree - strongly disagree

10. No man should refuse to enter the military service when drafted.
strongly agree - agree - undecided - disagree - strongly disagree

11. Everyone that is eligible should vote.
strongly agree - agree - undecided - disagree - strongly disagree

12. No one should be kept from holding a public office because of race, creed or color.
strongly agree - agree - undecided - disagree - strongly disagree

Section III

1. I just want to be called an American and nothing else, regarding nationality.
strongly agree - agree - undecided - disagree - strongly disagree

2. I consider myself to be just as American as anyone else.
strongly agree - agree - undecided - disagree - strongly disagree

3. I am proud to be called an American.
strongly agree - agree - undecided - disagree - strongly disagree

4. I identify with America.
strongly agree - agree - undecided - disagree - strongly disagree

5. I do not think of myself as an American.
   strongly agree - agree - undecided - disagree - strongly disagree

6. I feel that I am one with all white Anglo-Saxon Protestants in the United States.
   strongly agree - agree - undecided - disagree - strongly disagree

7. When foreigners insult Americans they are insulting me.
   strongly agree - agree - undecided - disagree - strongly disagree

8. The celebrations of America are my celebrations.
   strongly agree - agree - undecided - disagree - strongly disagree

9. I do not feel a close relationship with any other country except the United States.
   strongly agree - agree - undecided - disagree - strongly disagree

10. In the international competitions (i.e., Olympics) I always root for the United States to beat every other nation.
    strongly agree - agree - undecided - disagree - strongly disagree

11. I feel almost as close (or closer) a relationship with Mexico as with the United States.
    strongly agree - agree - undecided - disagree - strongly disagree

Section IV

1. The other students treat me like everyone else.
   strongly agree - agree - undecided - disagree - strongly disagree

2. I have never been rejected by anyone because of my nationality.
   strongly agree - agree - undecided - disagree - strongly disagree

3. No one has ever made fun of me or called me names because of my nationality or ancestors.
   strongly agree - agree - undecided - disagree - strongly disagree

4. There is no discrimination in San Antonio against people of my nationality or ancestry.
   strongly agree - agree - undecided - disagree - strongly disagree

5. My nationality has caused me problems.
   strongly agree - agree - undecided - disagree - strongly disagree

6. I am invited to as many parties as the rest of my classmates.
   strongly agree - agree - undecided - disagree - strongly disagree

7. In this city I am treated as well as anyone else.
   strongly agree - agree - undecided - disagree - strongly disagree

8. There is some discrimination against people of my religion here in San Antonio.
   strongly agree - agree - undecided - disagree - strongly disagree

In the following questions that require you to rank the answers, please place a 1 in the space before your first choice, a 2 before your second choice, and so on until all the spaces are filled out. If you honestly feel no preference, only check the space "no preference". If you feel the same about two or more groups give them the same rank.

1. Rank the following 1 through 5 in order of preference.

    _____Jew, _____Negro _____Mexican American, _____Anglo, _____Oriental,

    _____No Preference

2. Rank the following 1 through 5 in order of preference for picking a friend.

    _____Catholic, _____Jew, _____Protestant, _____Atheist, _____Other

    _____No Preference

3. Rank in order 1 through 8 the group that you prefer to pick your friends from.

    _____Anglo Protestant   _____Anglo Catholic

    _____Negro Protestant   _____Negro Catholic

    _____Oriental Protestant   _____Oriental Catholic

    _____Mexican American Protestant   _____Mexican American Catholic

    _____No Preference

4. Rank the following 1 through 5 in order of inferiority, or personal dislike. (1 signifies most inferior and 5 least inferior).

    _____Anglo, _____Negro, _____Jew, _____Oriental, _____Mexican American

    _____No Preference

5. People who go to public schools are usually better Americans than those who go to private schools.
    strongly agree - agree - undecided - disagree - strongly disagree

6. People who live in the United States should speak English all the time and not use some foreign language.
    strongly agree - agree - undecided - disagree - strongly disagree

7. I don't like people who go to private schools.
    strongly agree - agree - undecided - disagree - strongly disagree

8. A dark skinned person should not try to mix socially with whites.
    strongly agree - agree - undecided - disagree - strongly disagree

Section VI

1. List the <u>last names</u> of the girls (or boys) with whom you have had a date in the last year.

    _____

    _____

    _____

    _____   ____None

    _____

2. Please give the <u>last name</u> of your steady girlfriend (or boyfriend) if you have one, and any others you have ever had.

    _____

    _____

    _____

    _____   ____None

    _____

3. List the <u>last names</u> of all the girls (or boys) you know with whom you would like to have a date.

    _____

    _____

    _____

    _____   ____None

    _____

4. It's best for a person to date only those who are of the same nationality as he or she is.
   strongly agree - agree - undecided - disagree - strongly disagree

5. I will not restrict my selection of a spouse to one of my own nationality.
   strongly agree - agree - undecided - disagree - strongly disagree

6. I would like to marry an Anglo.
   strongly agree - agree - undecided - disagree - strongly disagree

7. I will probably marry a white Anglo Protestant.
   strongly agree - agree - undecided - disagree - strongly disagree

1. List the last names of your five best friends.

        _____

        _____

        _____

        _____

        _____

2. List the last names of your five best friends in your neighborhood.

        _____

        _____

        _____

        _____

        _____

3. List the last names of your five best friends at school.

        _____

        _____

        _____

        _____

        _____

4. List all the clubs, teams, groups or associations to which you belong.

        _____

        _____

        _____

        _____

5. List all the clubs, teams, groups or associations to which you belong that are limited in membership to one religion or one nationality.

        _____

        _____

        _____

THANK YOU

You have been selected to take part in a sociological study. Sociology is a science which studies human beings. This study in which you are asked to take part is a scientific study designed to discover what eighth graders in San Antonio think, feel and do in many different situations and on many issues.

So this is your chance to let people know how you feel as a group; it gives you the opportunity to express your personal opinions without fear that they may get you into trouble. No one will ever know what any of you answered as individuals. Only the overall group results will ever be made known, for example 70% said "yes," and 30% said "no."

Therefore, we ask your cooperation and complete honesty in answering the questionnaire which each of you will be given. As you will see, there is no place for your name, address or school, so no identification whatsoever will be possible.

Remember, there are no right or wrong answers to the questions, only true and false answers. An answer is false if it does not really reflect what you feel or do. Please make all your answers true.

In the last part of the questionnaire, there are several questions which require the last names of friends. We don't want first names because we don't want to identify anyone, but the last names are necessary because they allow us to identify nationalities. We are interested in seeing what nationalities tend to go around together most often. For example, do Irish go around more with other Irish or with Germans.

Please feel free to answer all of these questions also, because no one here at school or anyone else will ever see the names you list. Only the researcher will ever see these completed forms.

REFERENCES

Abbott, Walter M. (ed.)
    1966 The Documents of Vatican II. New York: Guild Press.

Asch, S. E.
    1956 "Studies of Independence and Conformity: I. A Minority of One Against
          a Unanimous Majority." Psychological Monographs 70 (9):1-70.

Beloff, Halla
    1958 "Two Forms of Social Conformity: Aquiescence and Conventionality,"
          Journal of Abnormal and Social Psychology 56 (1):99-104.

Berry, Brewton
    1965 Race and Ethnic Relations. Boston: Houghton Mifflin Co.

Blumer, Herbert
    1961 "Race Prejudice as a Sense of Group Position." Pp. 217-227 in J. Masuoka
          and Preston Valien (eds.), Race Relations, Problems, and Theory. Chapel
          Hill: University of North Carolina Press.

Blumer, Herbert
    1955 "Reflections on Theory of Race Relations." Pp. 3-21 in Andrew W. Lind
          (ed.), Race Relations in World Perspective. Honolulu: University of
          Hawaii Press.

Bogardus, Emory S.
    1930 "Race Relations Cycle." American Journal of Sociology 35 (4):612-617.

Bressler, Marvin and Charles Westoff
    1963 "Catholic Education, Economic Values, and Achievement." American Journal
          of Sociology 69 (3):225-233.

Broom, Leonard and Eshref Shevky
    1952 "Mexicans in the United States: A Problem of Social Differentiation."
          Sociology and Social Research 36 (1):150-158.

Brown, W. O.
    1934 "Culture Contact and Race Conflict." Pp. 34-37 in E. B. Reuter (ed.),
          Race and Culture Contacts. New York: McGraw-Hill Book Company.

Callahan, Raymond E.
    1958 An Introduction to Education in American Society. New York: Alfred A.
          Knopf.

D'Antonio, William V. and Julian Samora
    1962 "Occupational Stratification in Four Southwestern Communities." Social
          Forces 41 (1):17-25.

Demerath III, N.J. and Philip E. Hammond
    1969 Religion in Social Context. New York: Random House.

De Young, Chris A. and Richard Wynn
    1972 American Education. New York: McGraw-Hill Book Company.

Educational Policies Commission
    1962 The Central Purpose of American Education. Washington, D.C.: National
          Education Association.

Edwards, Allen L.
    1957 Techniques of Attitude Scale Construction. New York: Appleton-Century-
          Crofts, Inc.

Forbes, Jack D.
    1970 "Mexican Americans." Pp. 7-16 in John H. Burma (ed.), Mexican Americans
          in the United States. Cambridge: Schenkman Publishing Company, Inc.

Galarza, Ernesto
    1970 "La Mula No Nacio Arisca." Pp. 199-206 in John H. Burma (ed.), Mexican
          Americans in the United States. Cambridge: Schenkman Publishing Company,
          Inc.

Glick, Clarence B.
    1955 "Social Roles and Types in Race Relations." Pp. 239-241 in Andrew W. Lind
          (ed.), Race Relations in World Perspective. Honolulu: University of
          Hawaii Press.

Gordon, Milton
    1964 Assimilation in American Life. New York: Oxford University Press.

Gray, William S. (ed.)
    1934 General Education: Its Nature, Scope and Essential Elements. Proceedings
          of the Institute for Administrative Officers of Higher Institutions, Vol.
          VI. Chicago: University of Chicago Press.

Grebler, Leo, Joan W. Moore and Ralph C. Guzman
    1970 The Mexican American People. New York: The Free Press.

Greeley, Andrew M.
    1973 "Public and Nonpublic Schools--Losers Both." School Review 81 (2):195-206.

Heller, Celia S.
    1966 Mexican American Youth: Forgotten Youth at the Crossroad. New York:
          Random House.

Herberg, Will
    1955 Protestant-Catholic-Jew. New York: Doubleday and Company, Inc.

Horton, Paul and Chester Hunt
    1972 Sociology. Third edition. New York: McGraw-Hill Book Company.

Howard, John R.
    1970 Awakening Minorities. New York: Transaction Books.

Husslein, Joseph (ed.)
    1942 "Encyclical on Christian Education of Youth." Social Wellsprings, Vol. II.
          Milwaukee: The Bruce Publishing Company.

Janis, I. L. and P. B. Field
    1959 "Sex Differences and Personality Factors Related to Persuasibility." Pp.
          55-68 in C. I. Hovland and I. L. Janis (eds.), Personality and Persuasibility.
          New Haven: Yale University Press.

Johnson, James A., John Johansen, Victor Dupuis and Harold Collins
    1969 Introduction to the Foundations of American Education. Boston: Allyn and
          Bacon, Inc.

Kerlinger, Fred N.
    1964 Foundations of Behavioral Research. New York: Holt, Rinehart and Winston.

Kohn, Melvin L.
    1969 Class and Conformity. Homewood, Ill.: The Dorsey Press.

Kuvlesky, William and Victoria Patella
    1971 "Degree of Ethnicity and Aspirations for Upward Social Mobility Among
          Mexican American Youth." Journal of Vocational Behavior 1 (3):231-244.

Kuvlesky, William, David Wright and Rumaldo Juarez
    1971 "Status Projections and Ethnicity: A Comparison of Mexican American,
          Negro, and Anglo Youth." Journal of Vocational Behavior 1 (2):137-151.

Labovitz, Sanford
    1967 "Some Observations on Measurement of Statistics." Social Forces 46 (2):
          151-160.

Lenski, Gerhard
    1967 "Religion's Impact on Secular Institutions." Pp. 217-236 in Joan Brothers
          (ed.), Readings in the Sociology of Religion. London: Pergamon Press, Ltd.

Lieberson, Stanley
    1961 "A Societal Theory of Race and Ethnic Relations." American Sociological
          Review 26 (6):902-910.

Lindzey, Gardner and Elliot Aronson
    1969 The Handbook of Social Psychology. Reading, Mass.: Addison-Wesley Publish-
          ing Company.

Marlowe, David and Kenneth Gergen
    1969 "Personality and Social Interaction." Pp. 590-665 in Gardner Lindzey and
          Elliot Aronson (eds.), Handbook of Social Psychology. Reading, Mass.:
          Addison-Wesley Publishing Company.

Madus, George E. and Roger Linnan
    1973 "The Outcome of Catholic Education." School Review 81 (2):207-228.

McGucken, William J.
    n.d. Catholic Education. New York: The American Press.

Mittlebach, Frank G. and Joan W. Moore
    1968 "Ethnic Endogamy: The Case of the Mexican American." American Journal of
          Sociology 74 (1):50-62.

Monroe, Paul
    1913 Cyclopedia of Education. New York: The MacMillan Company.

Moore, Joan W.
    1970 Mexican Americans. Englewood Cliffs, N.J.: Prentice Hall, Inc.